LITTLE DINOSAUR

COPY COLORING BOOK FOR KIDS

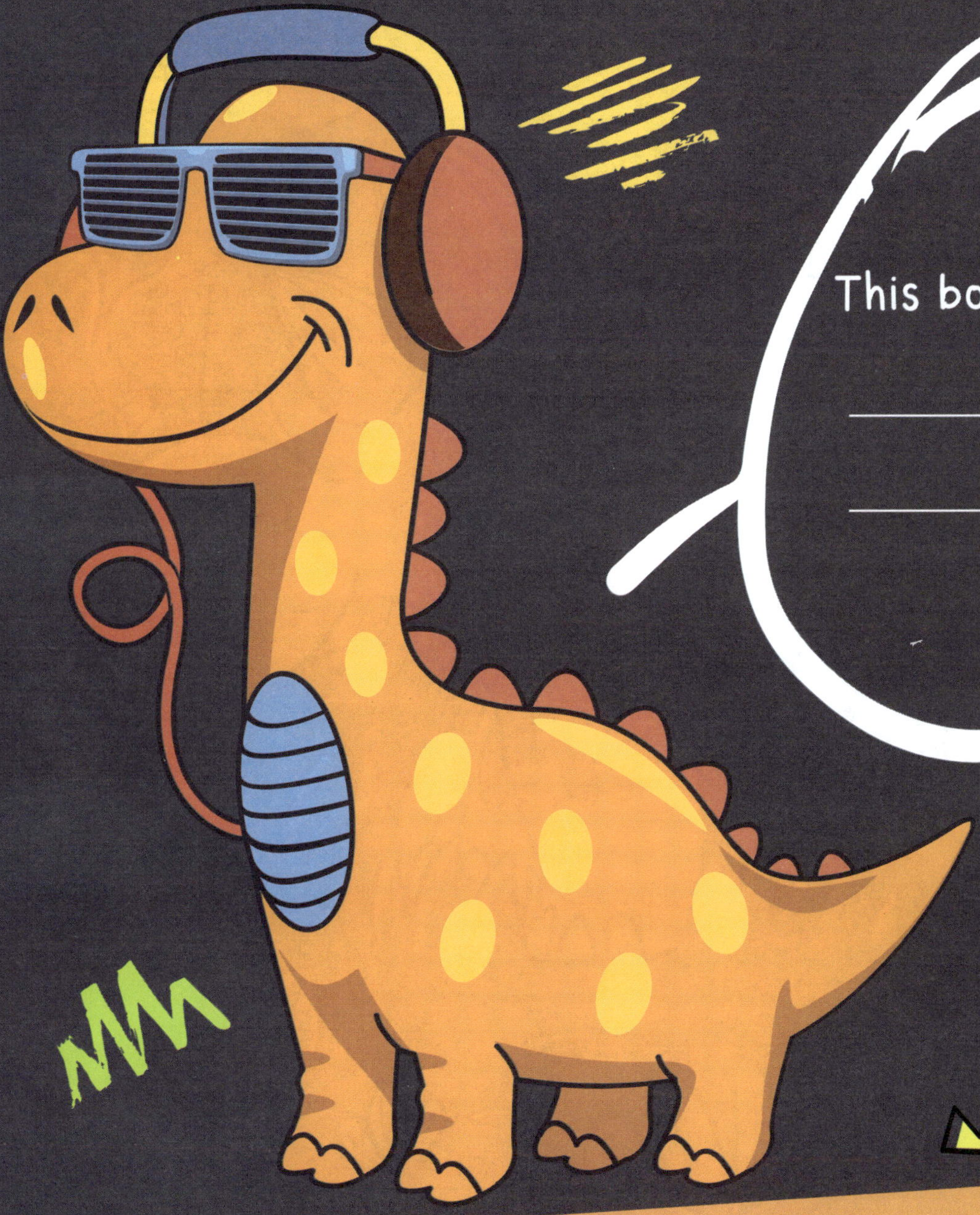

This book belongs to

____

____

Wonder House

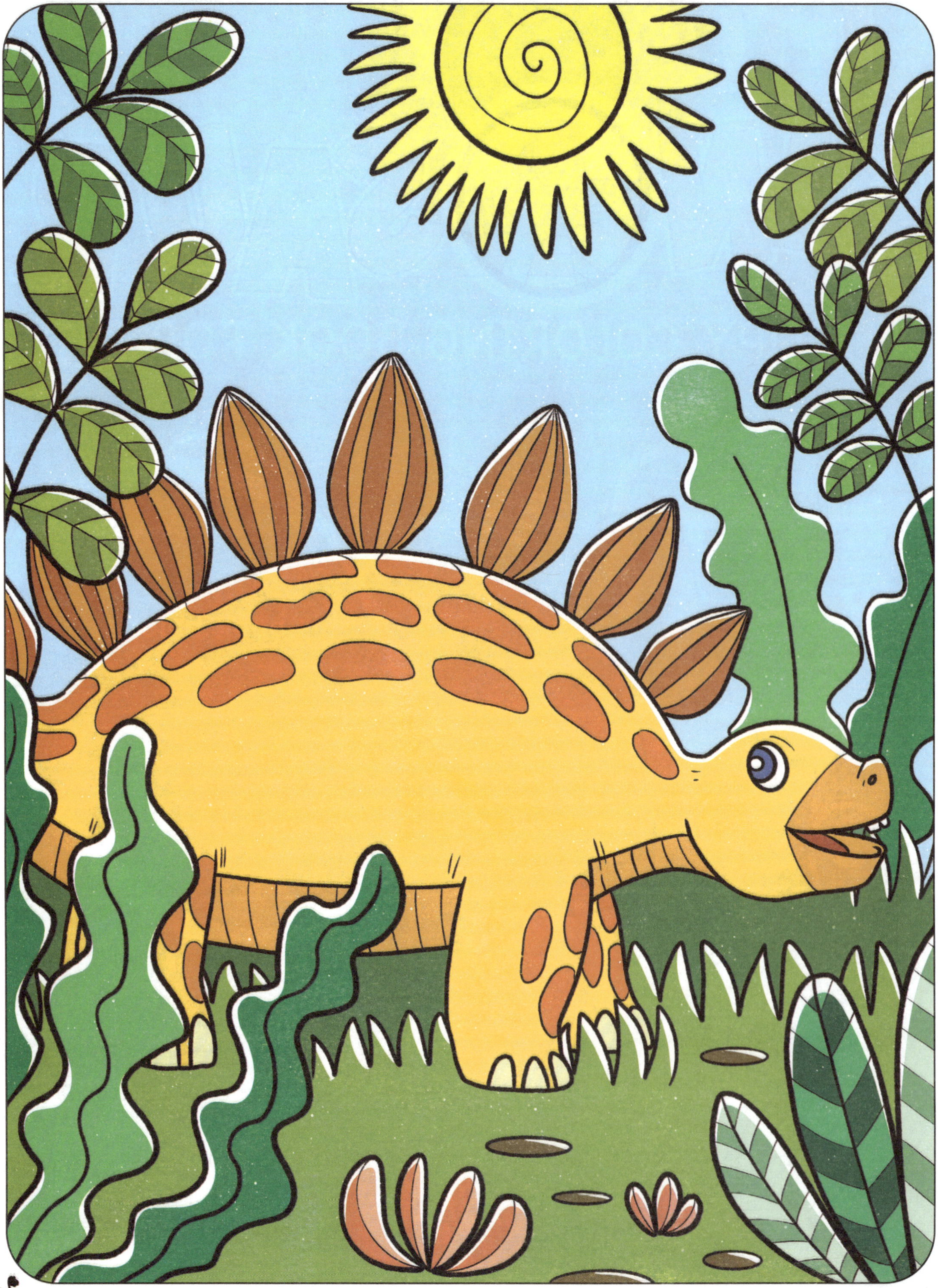

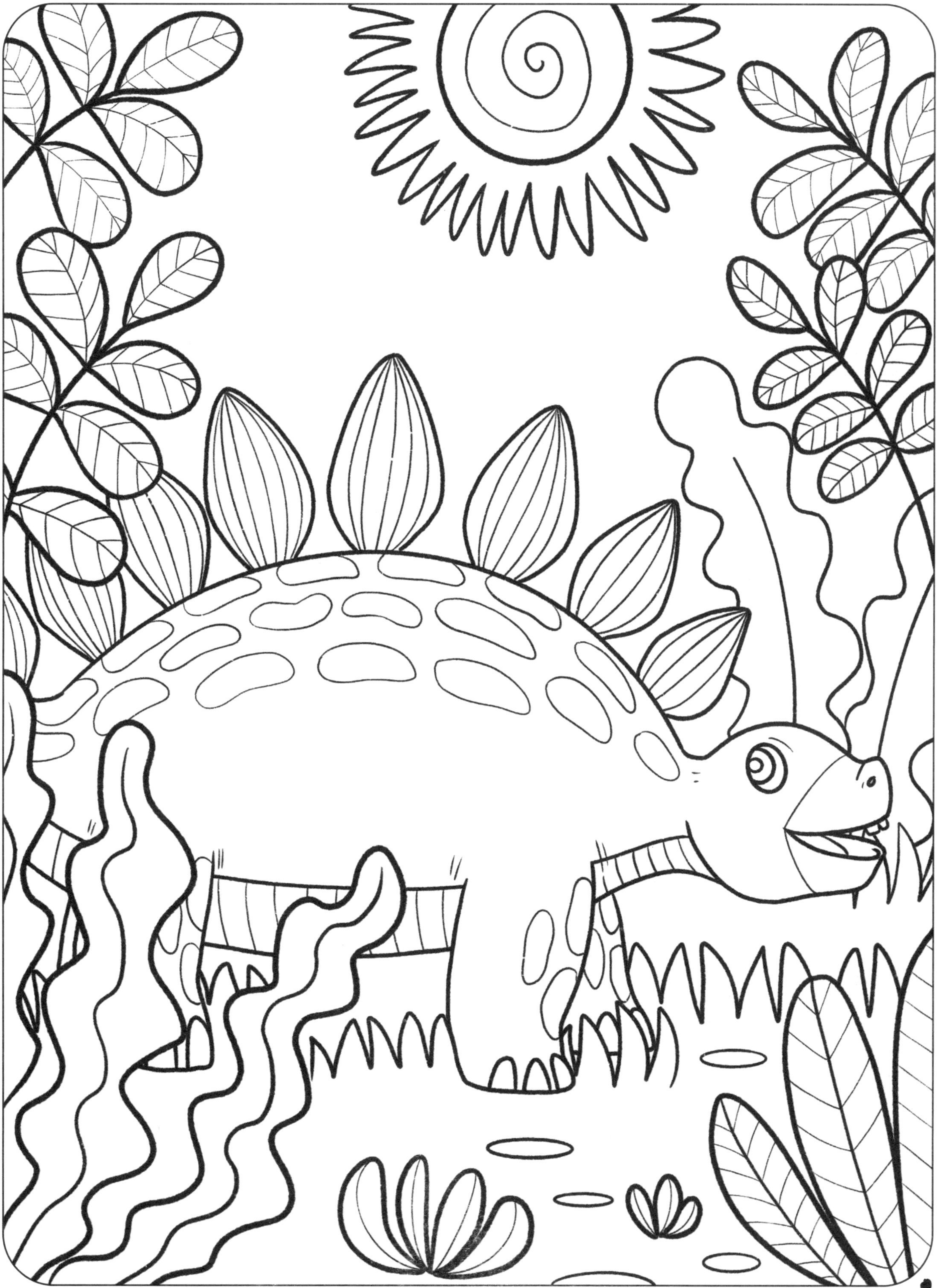

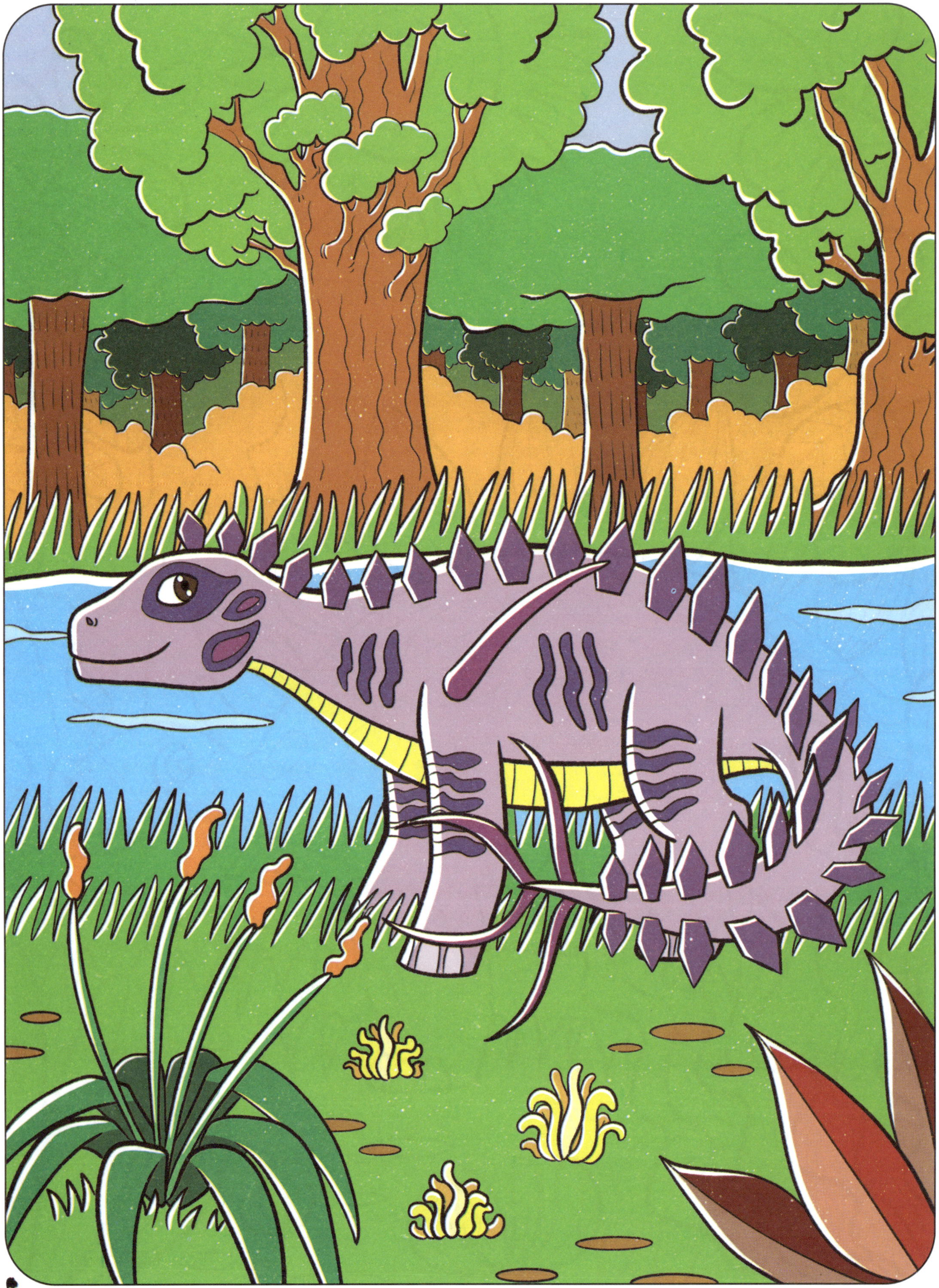

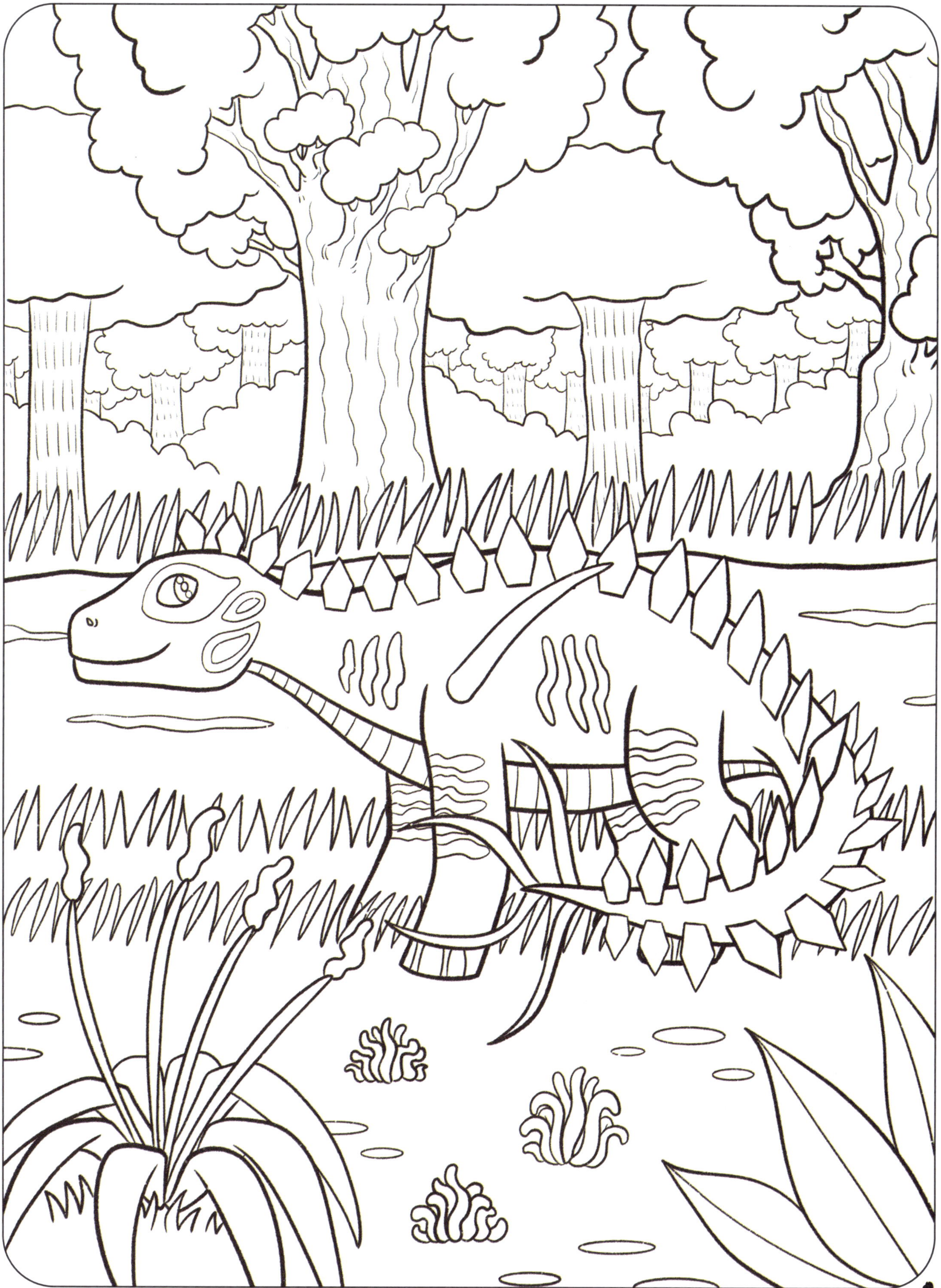

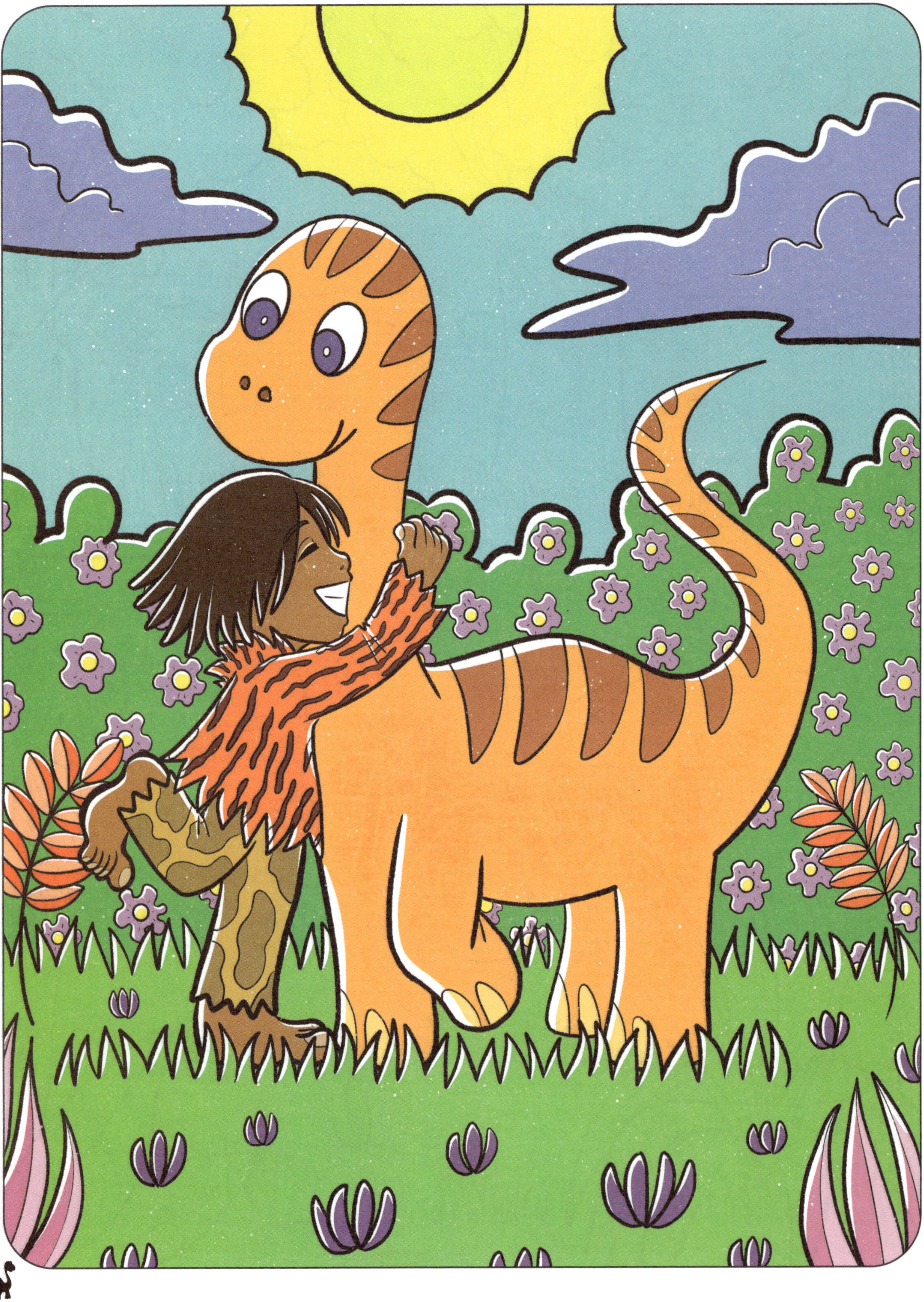

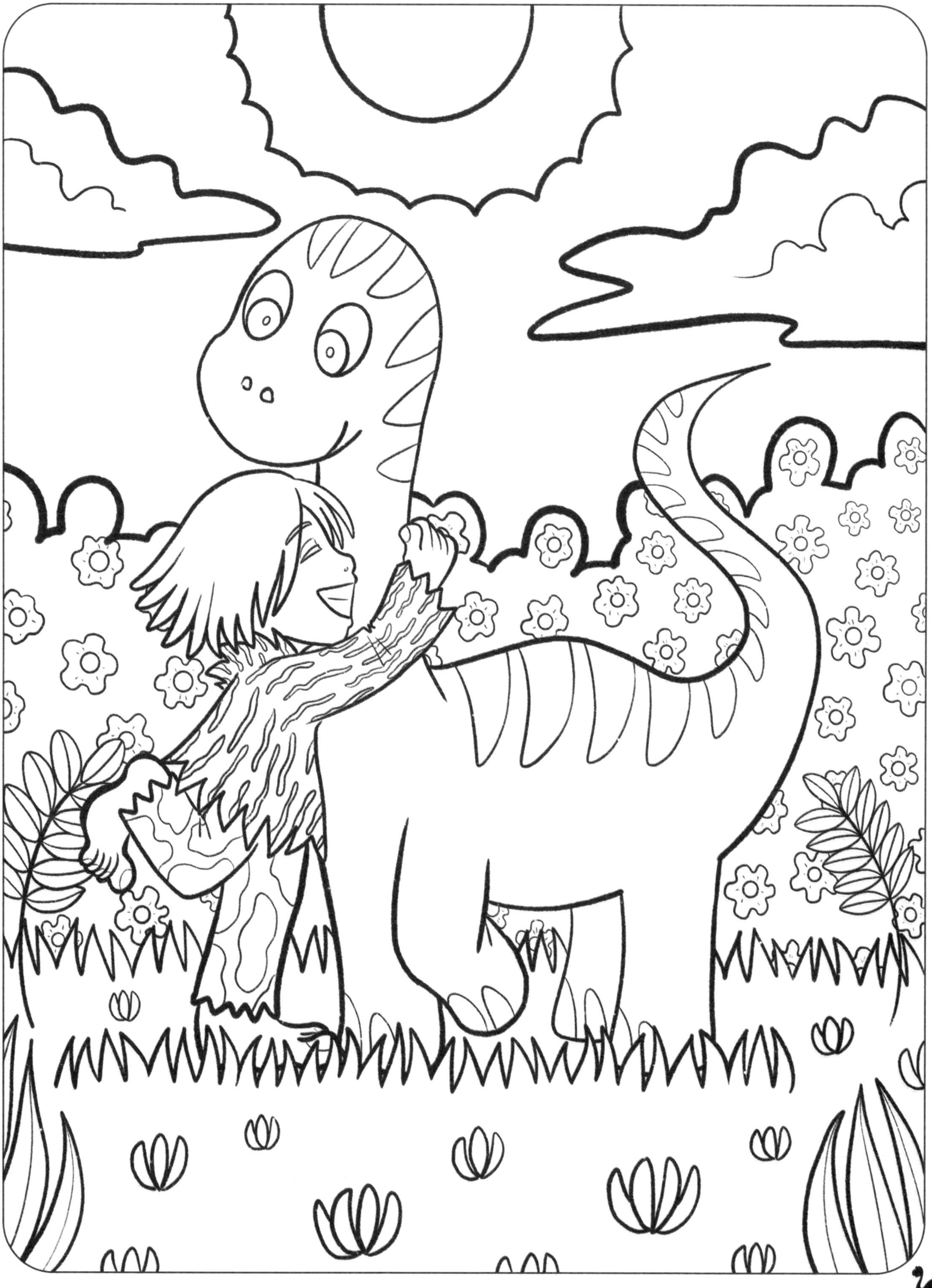

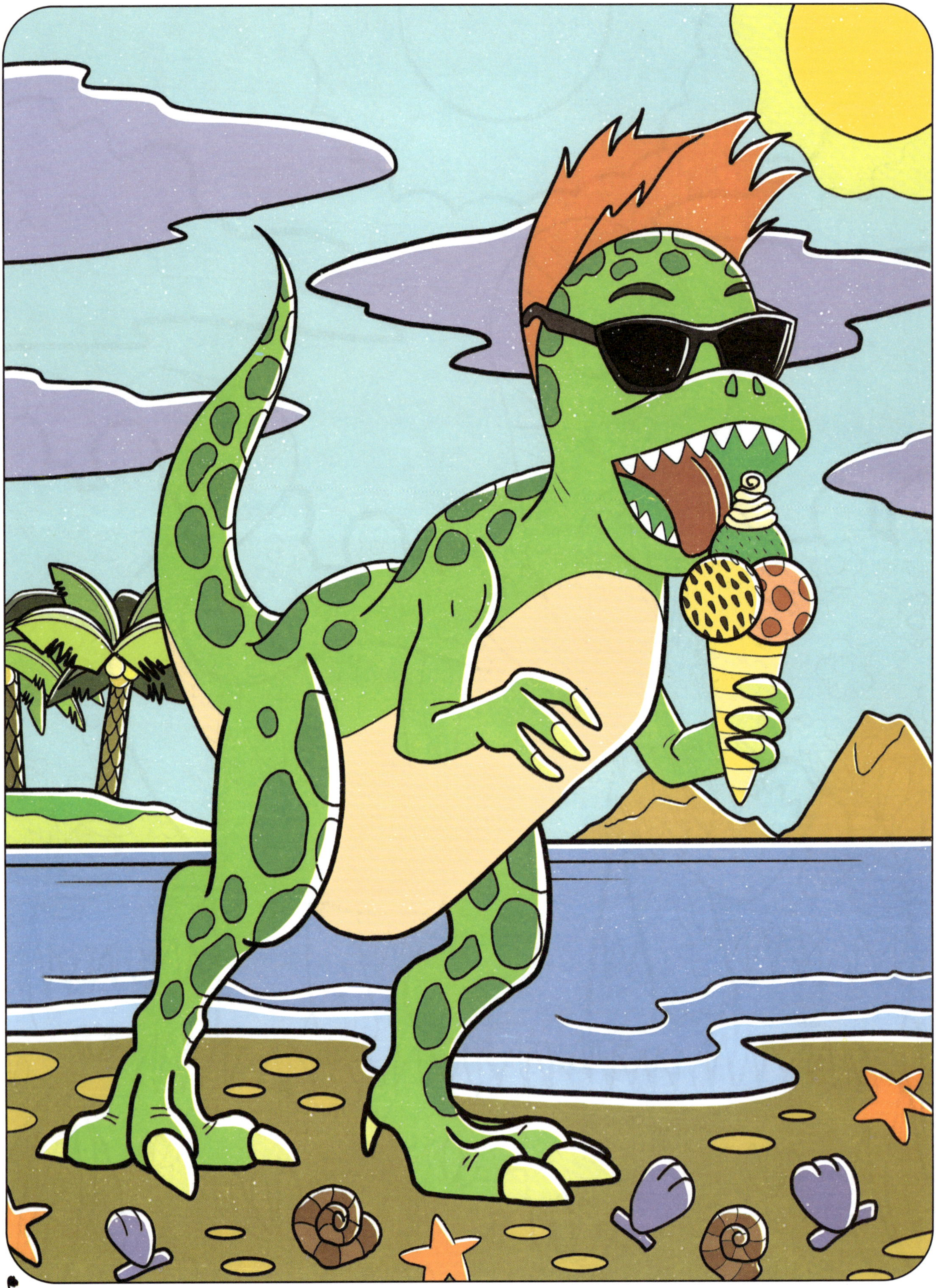

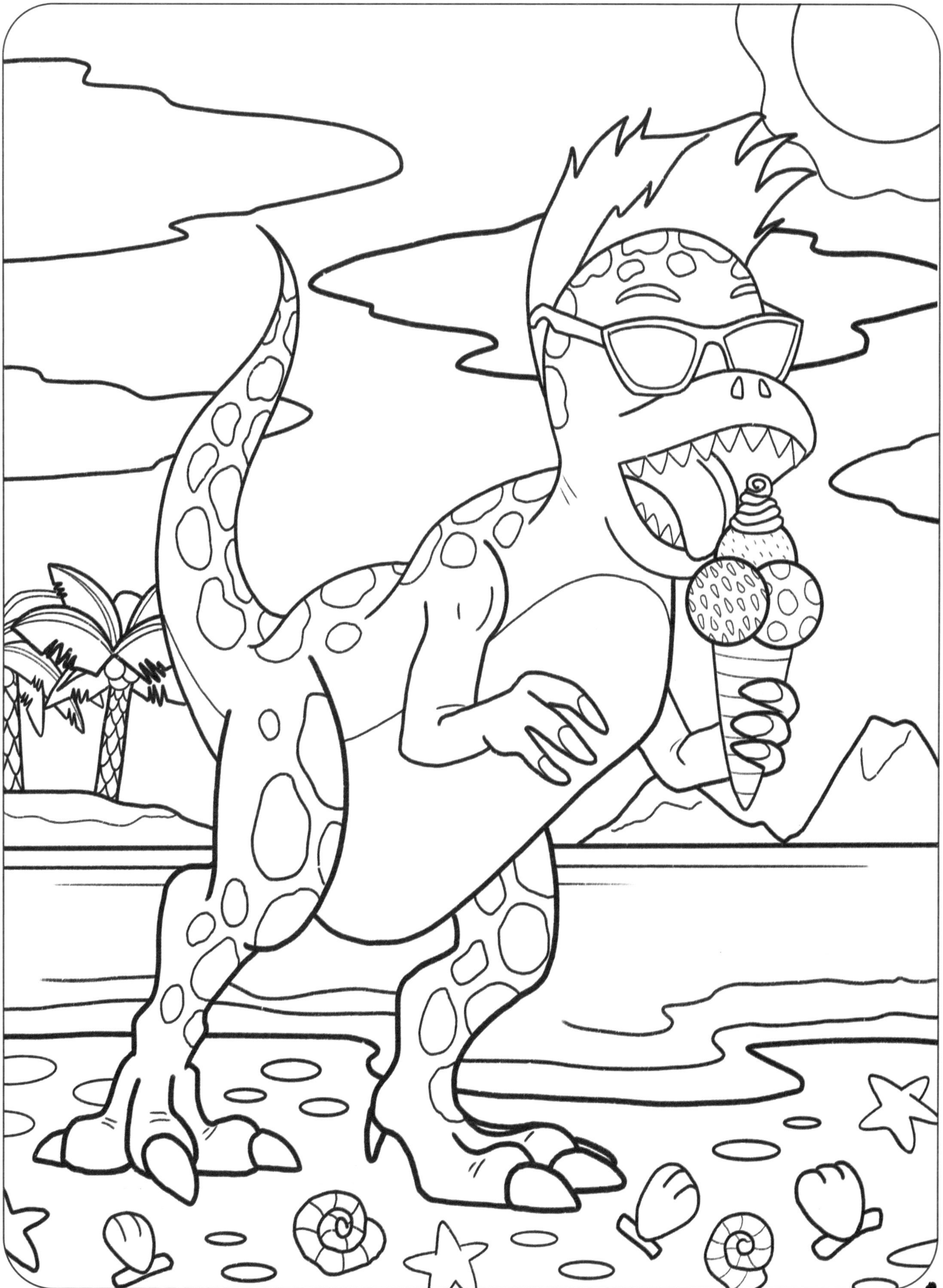

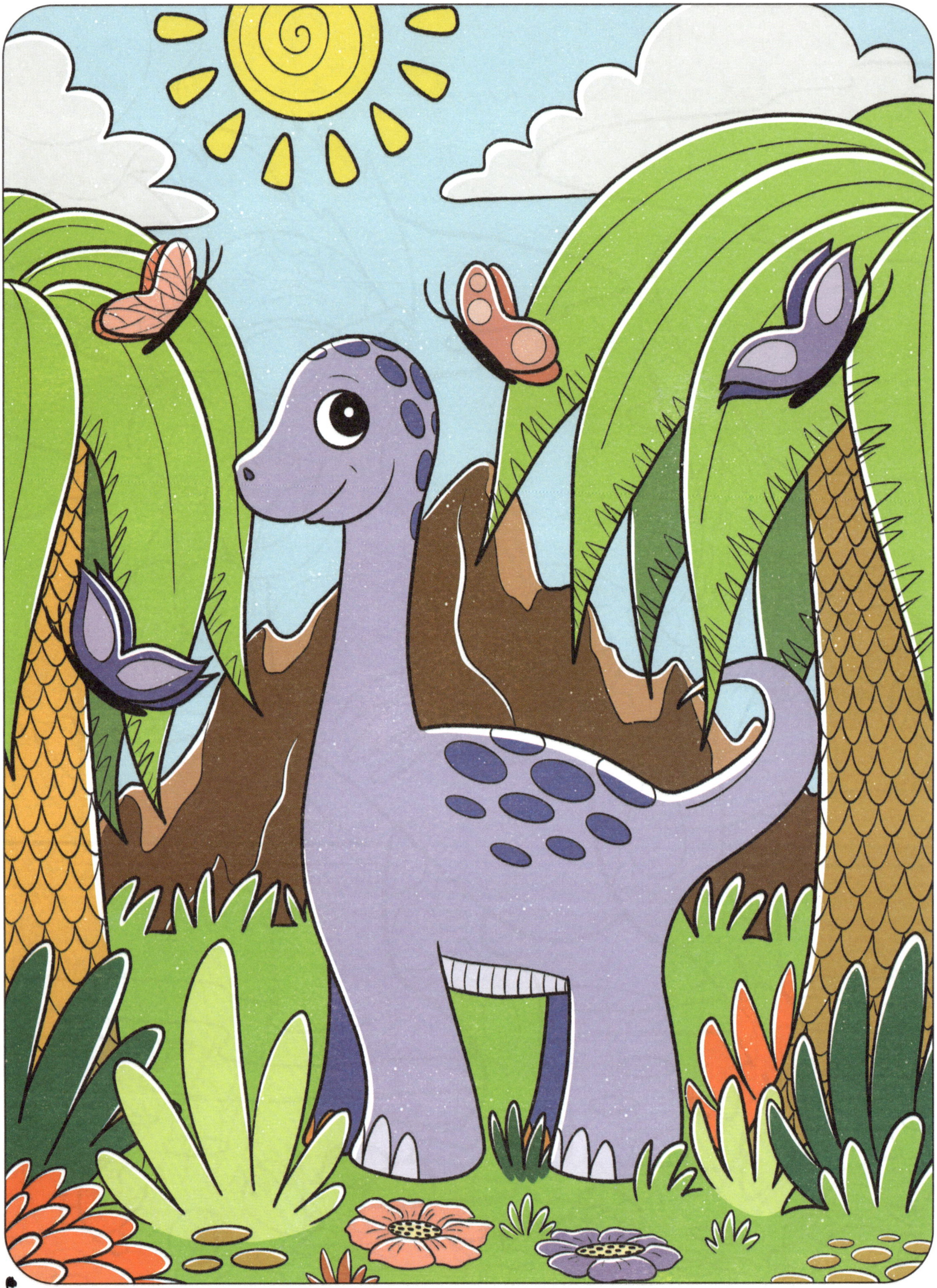

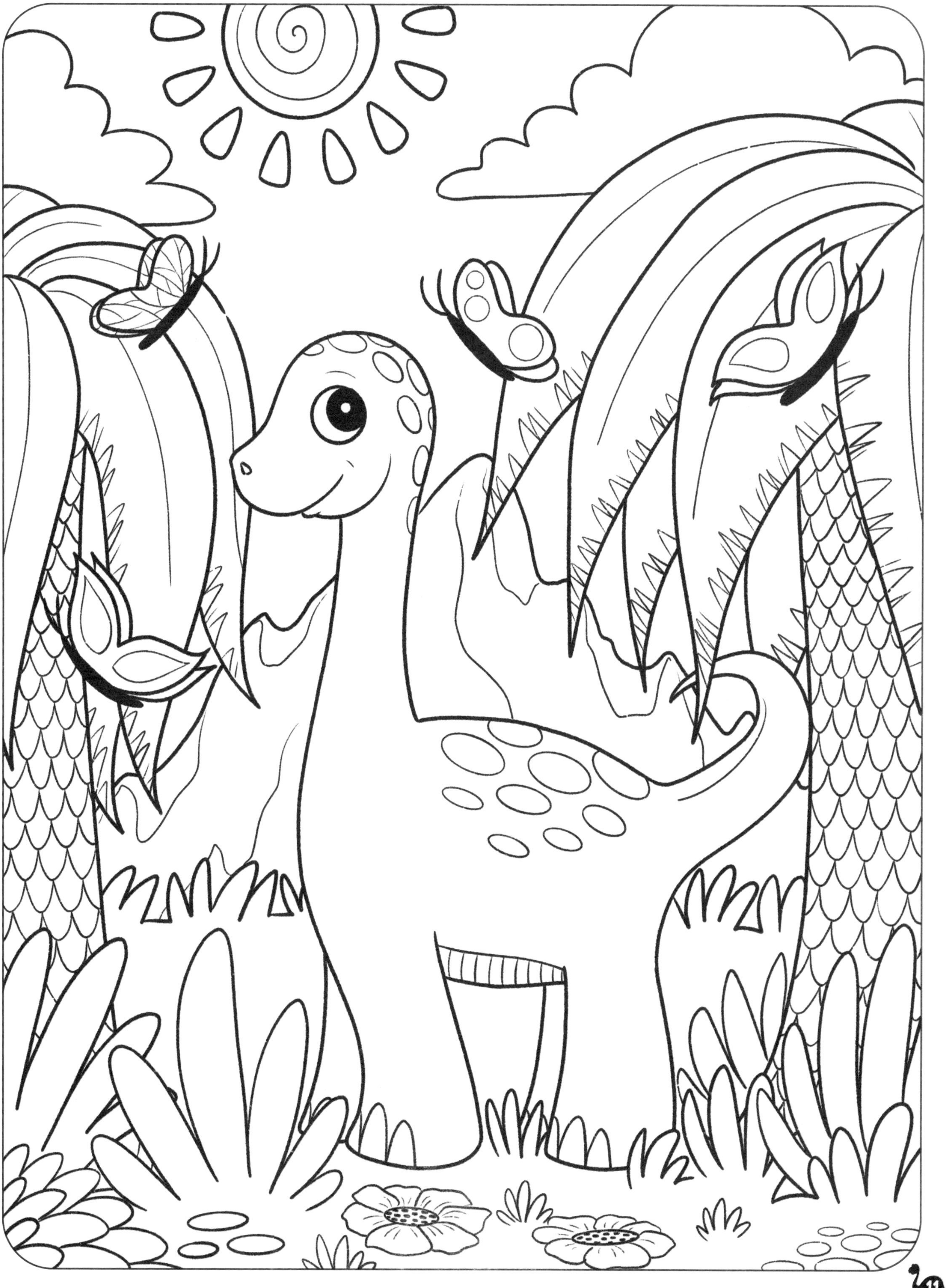

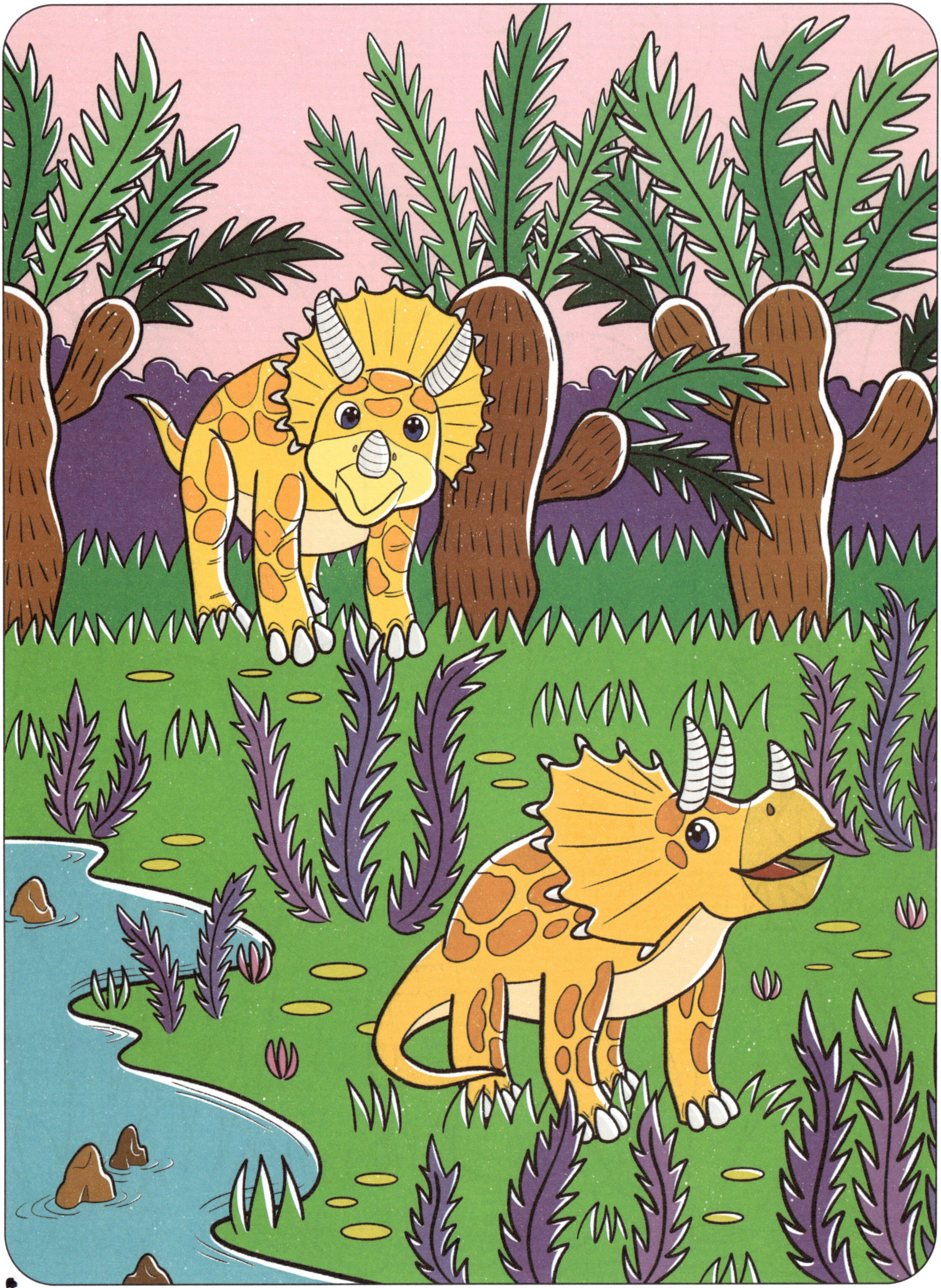

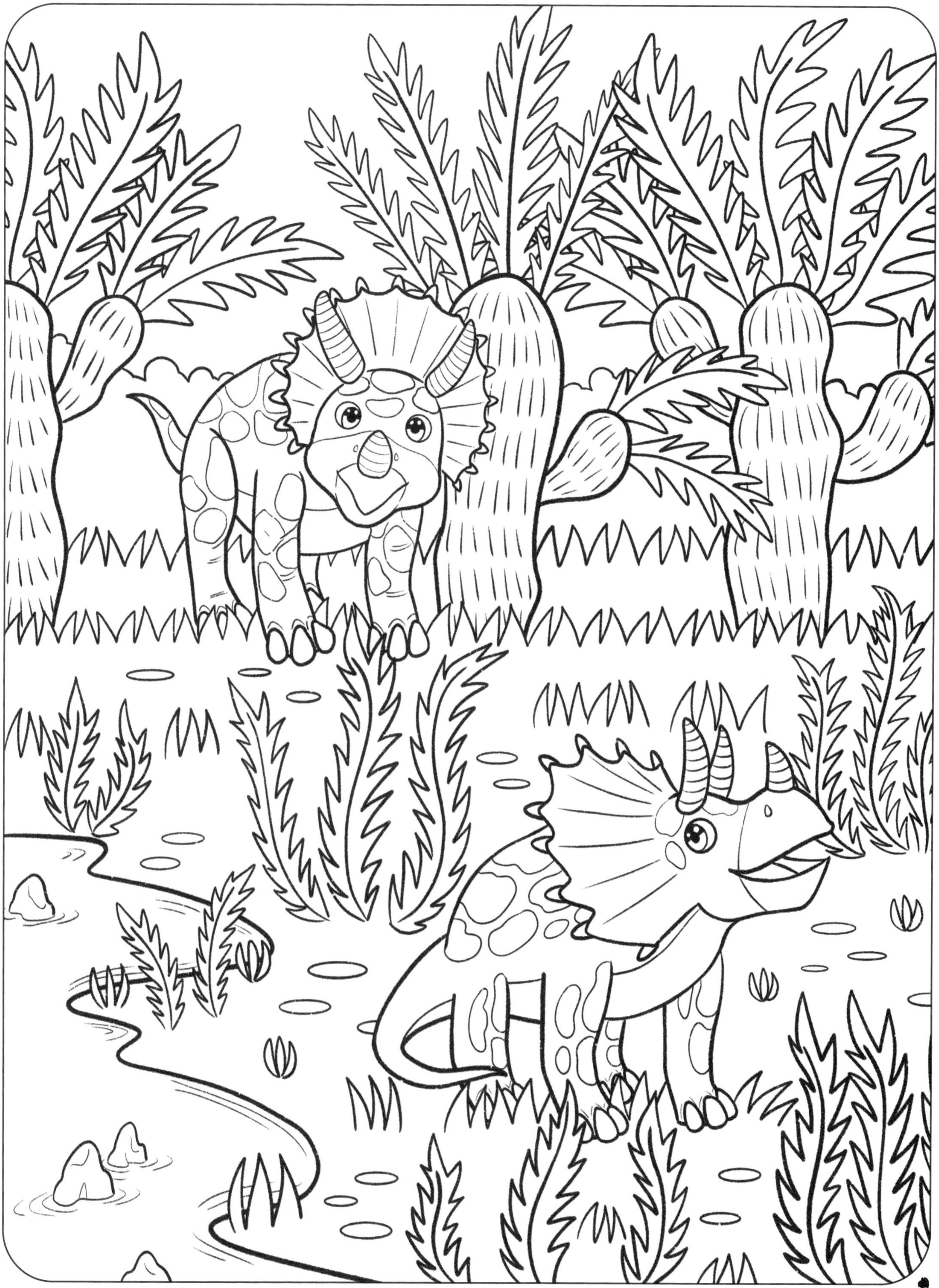

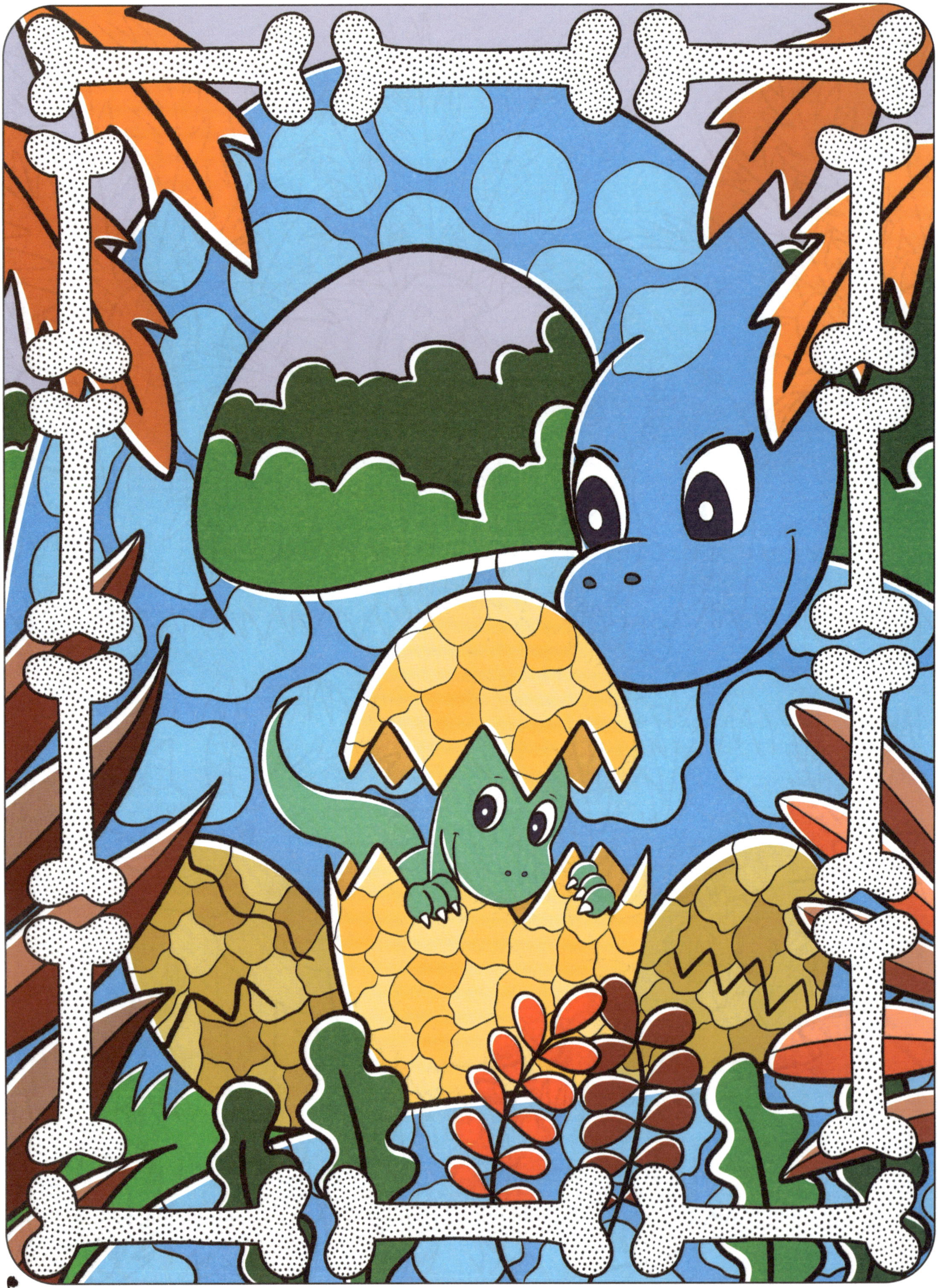

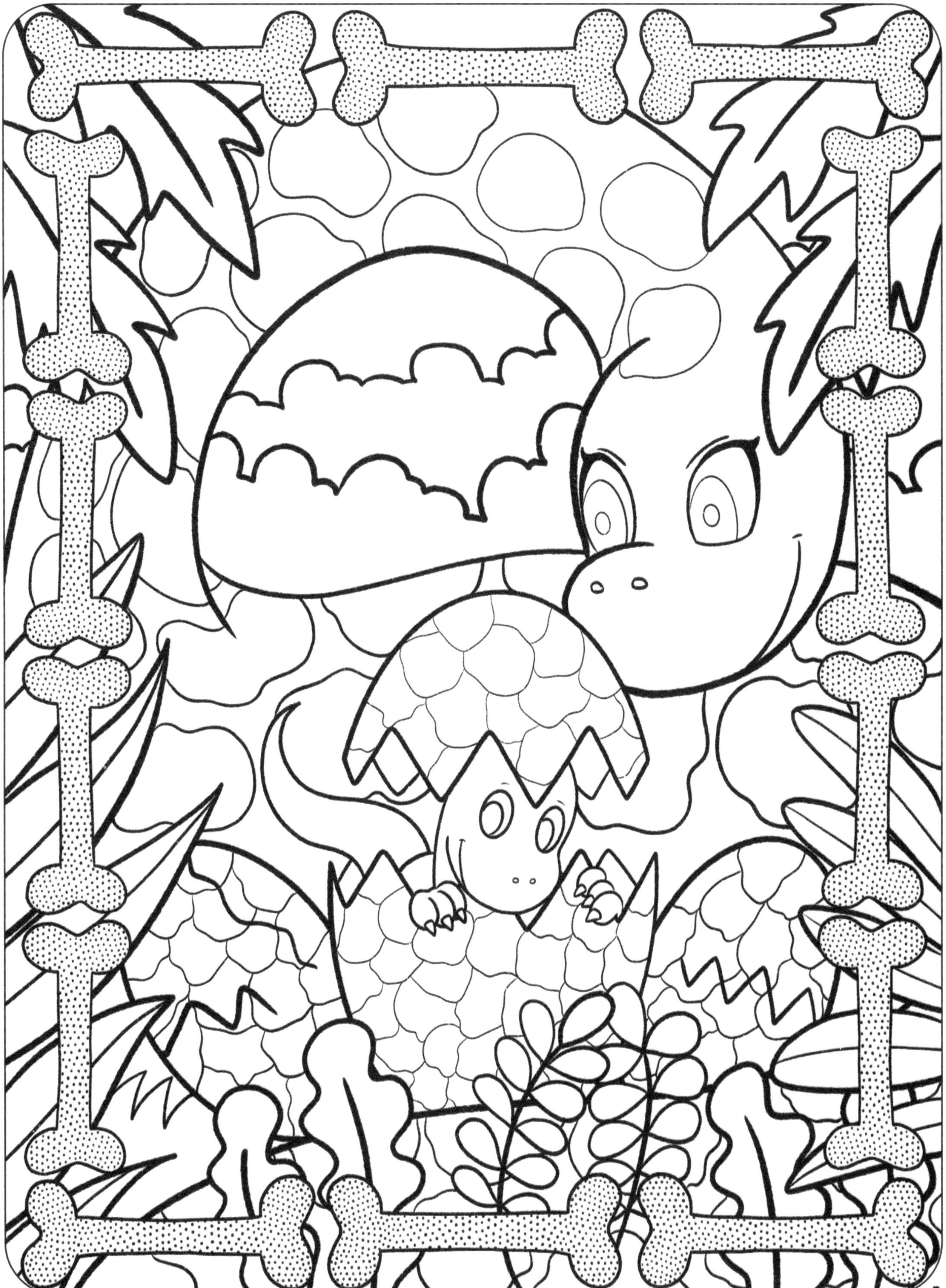

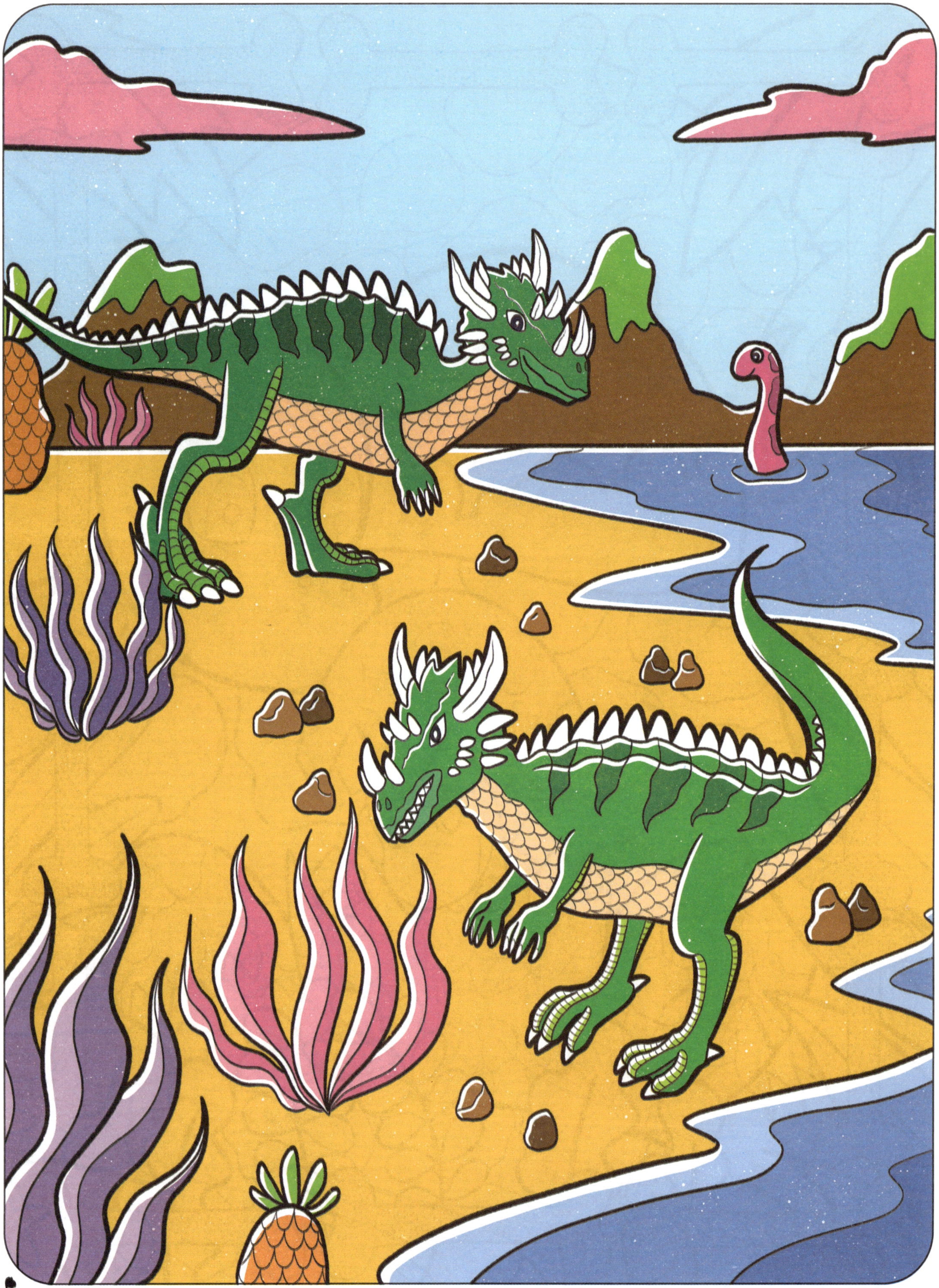

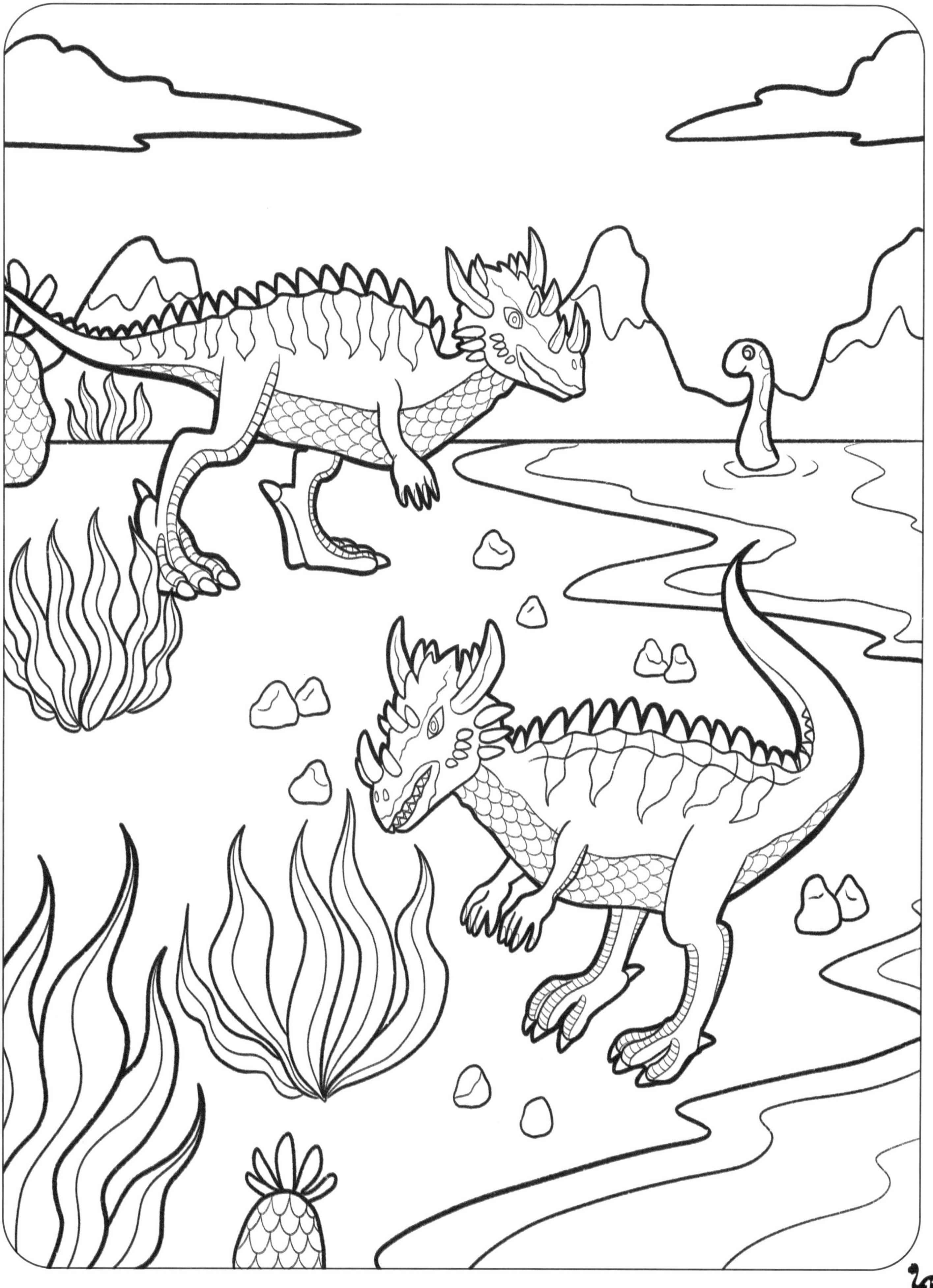

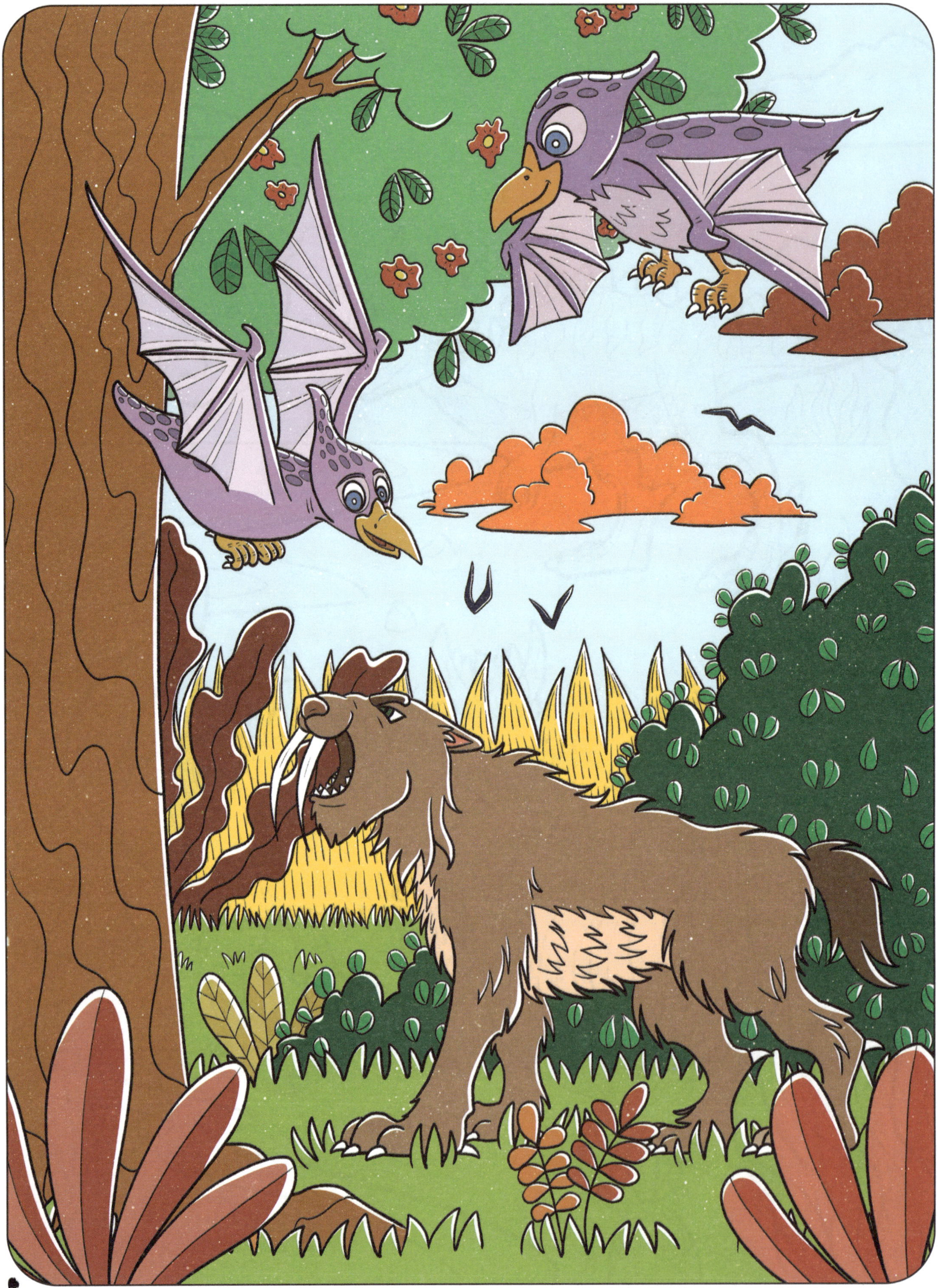

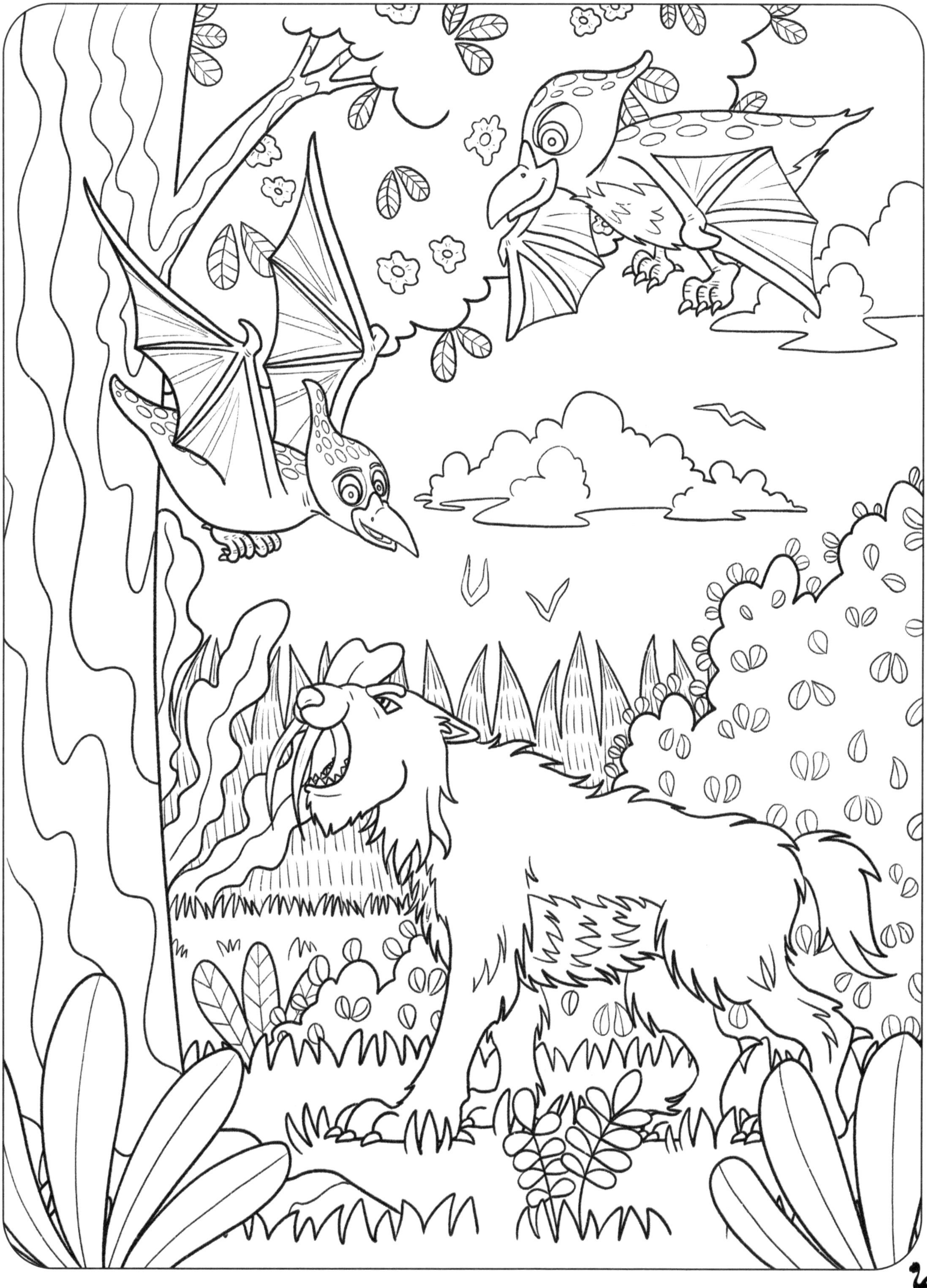

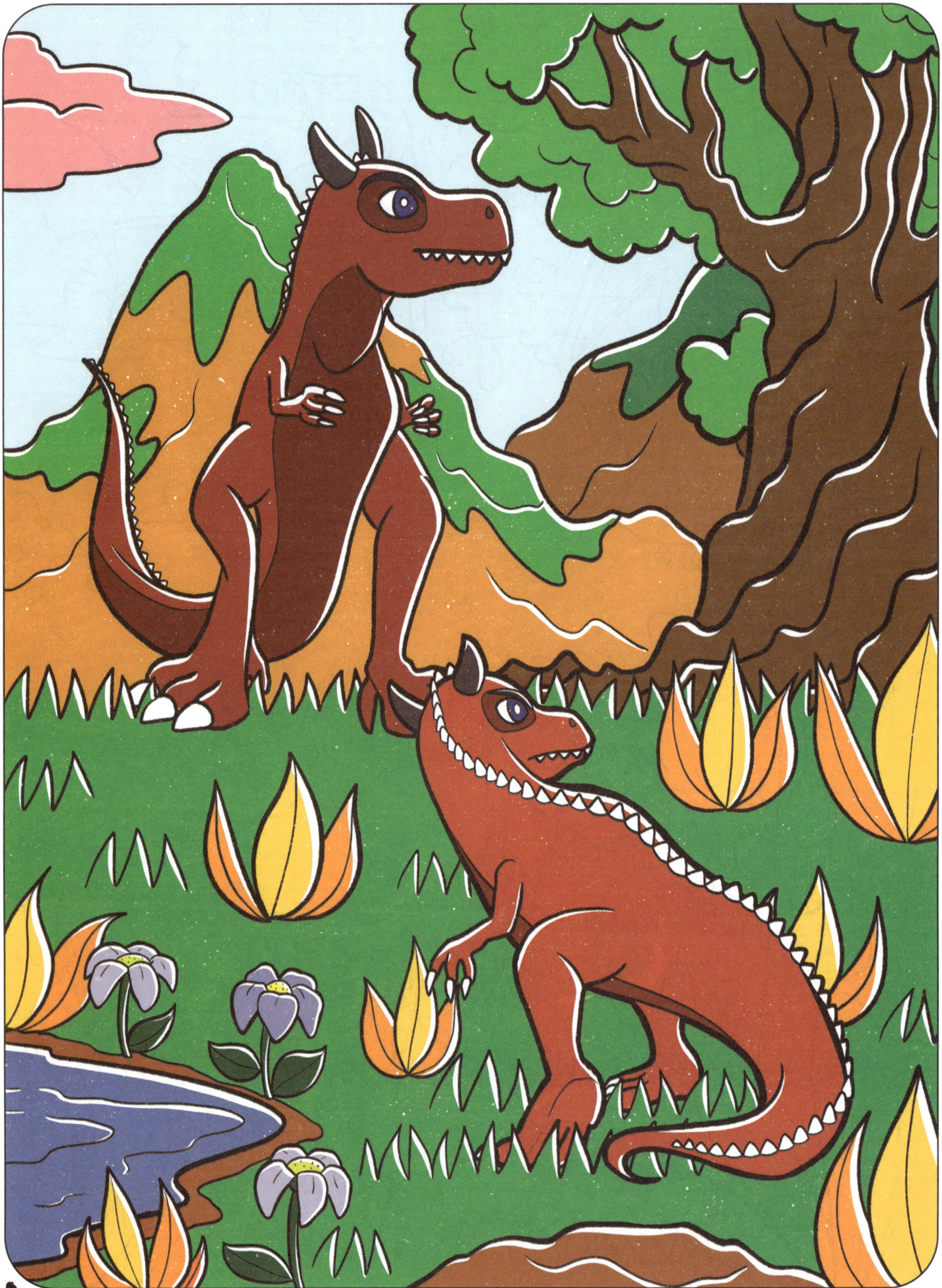

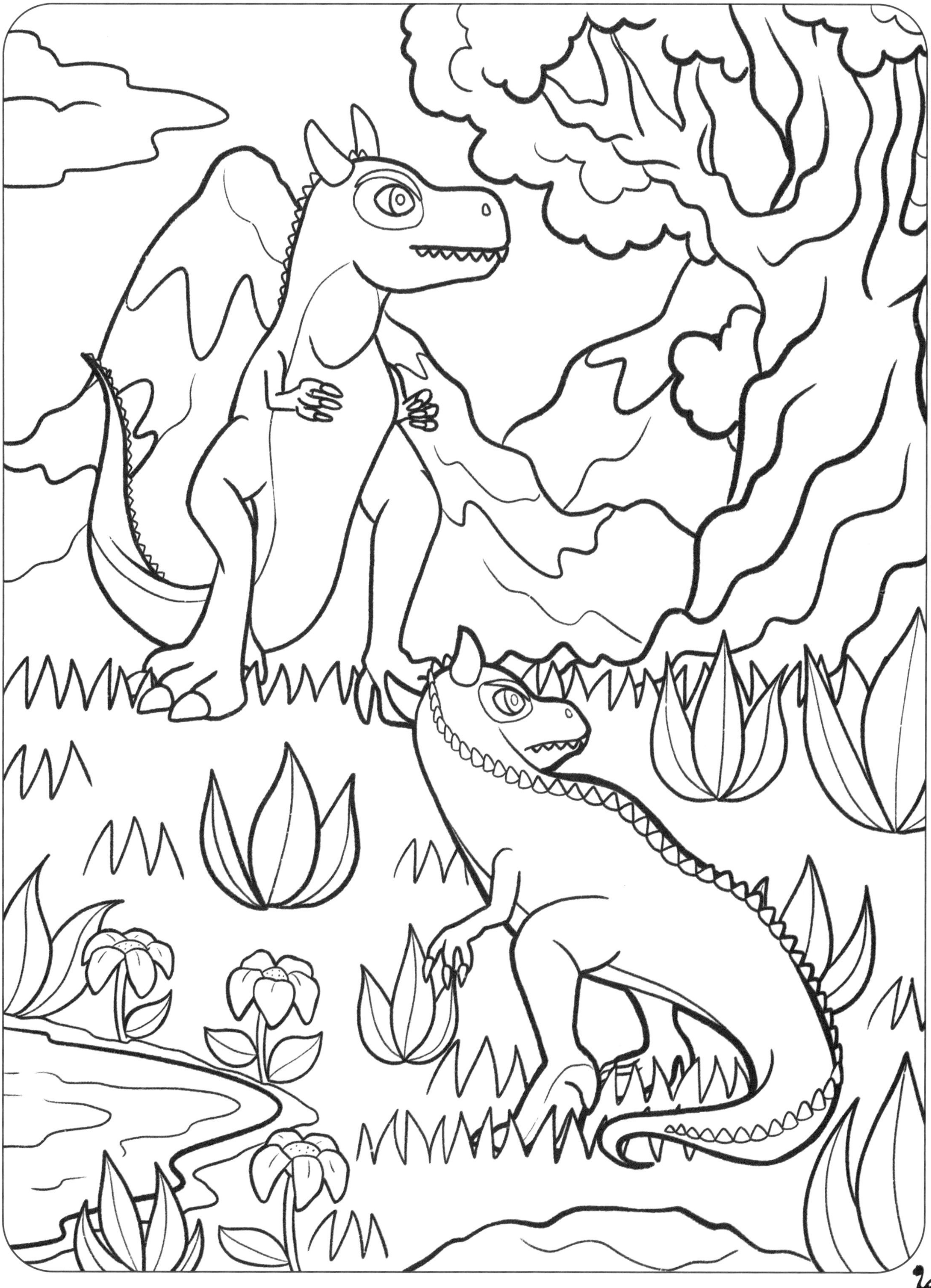

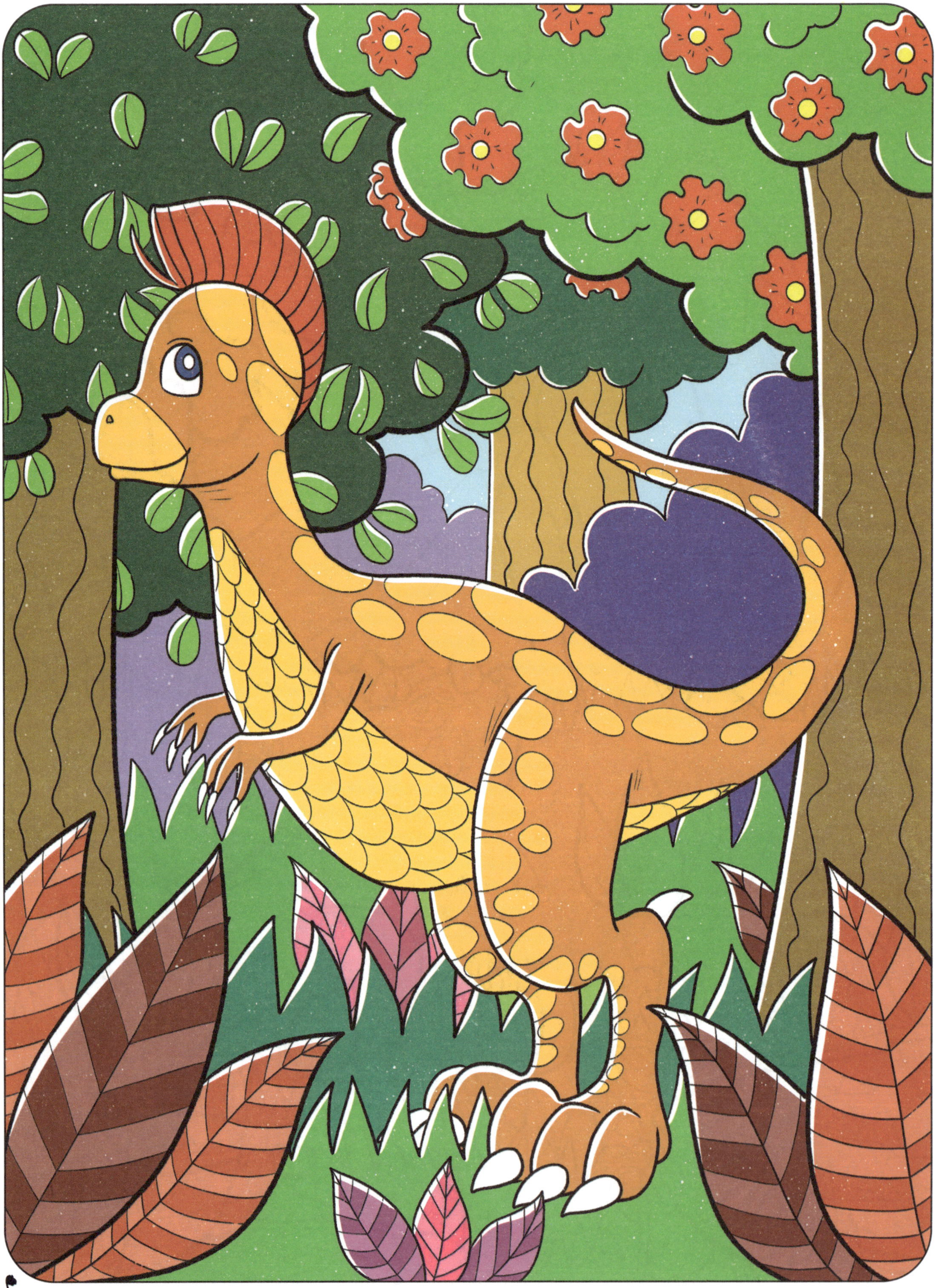

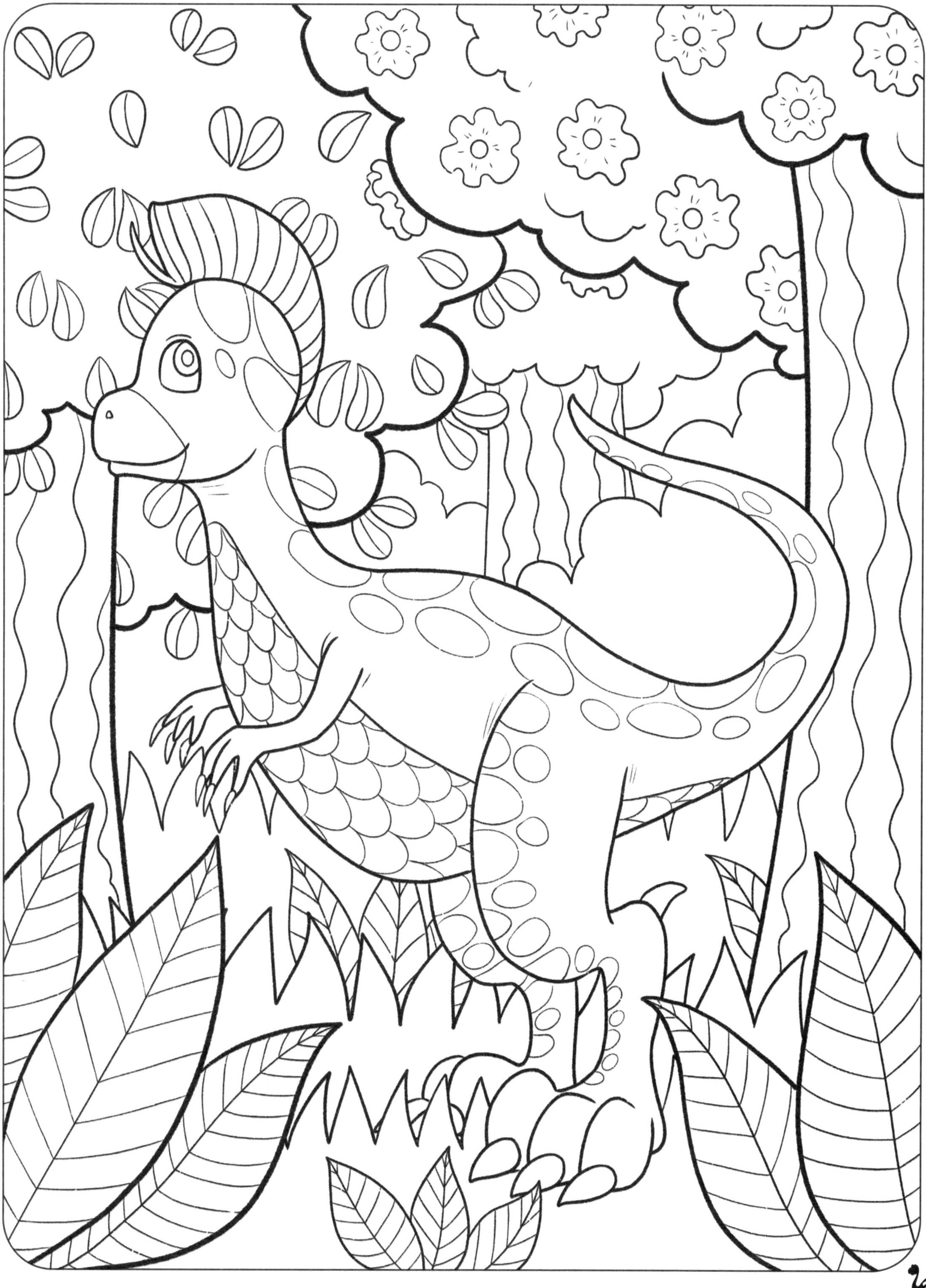

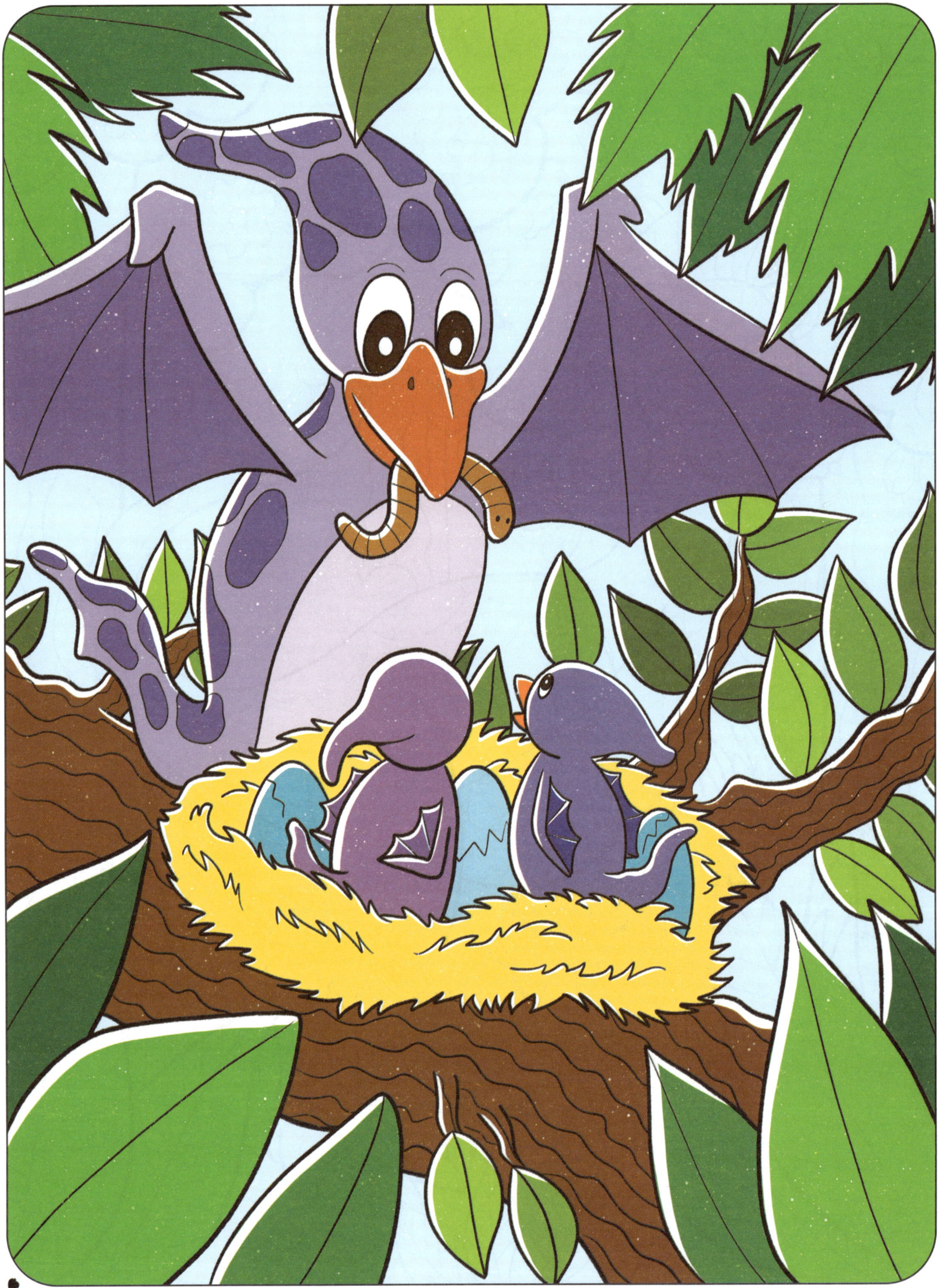

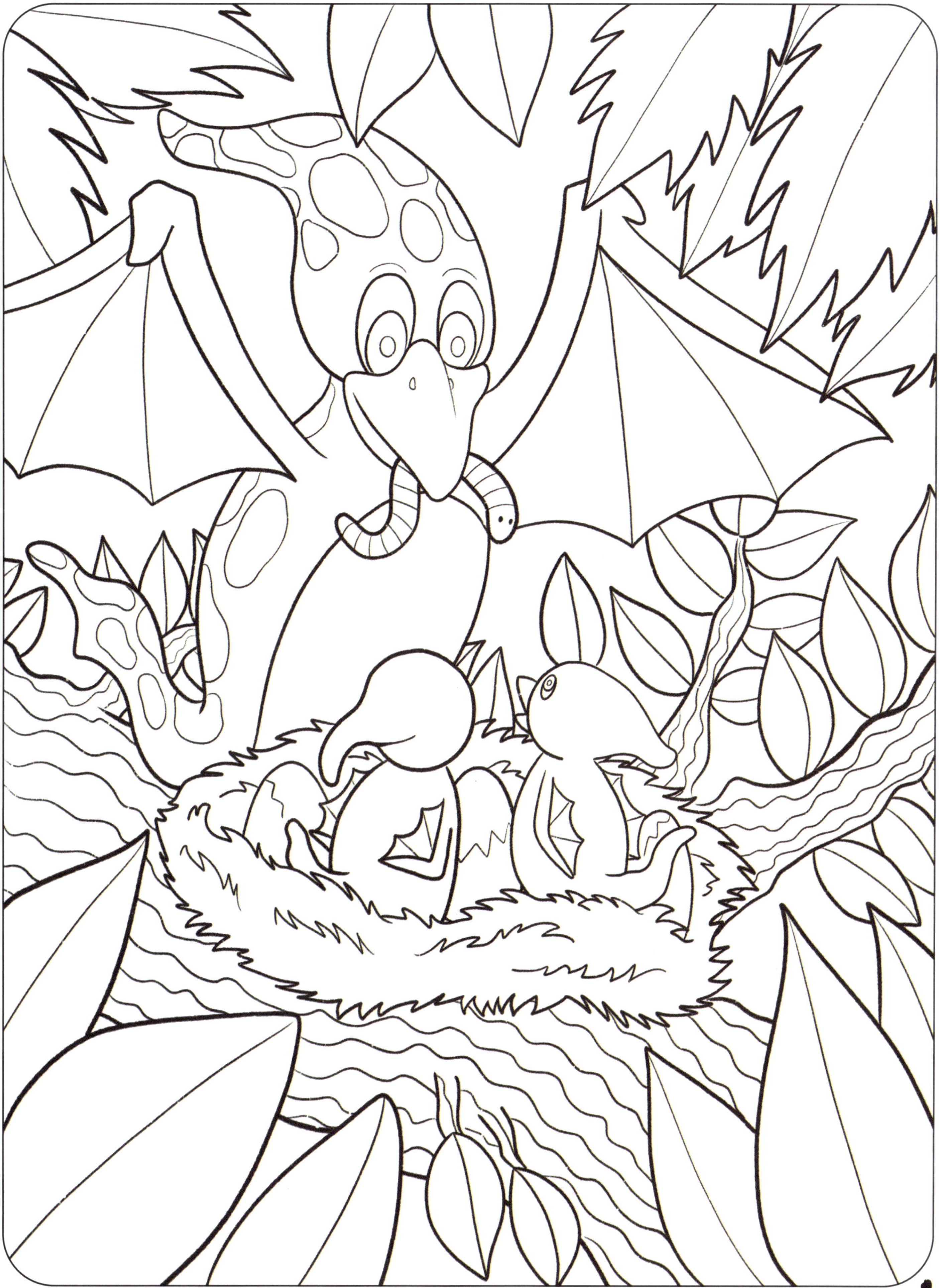

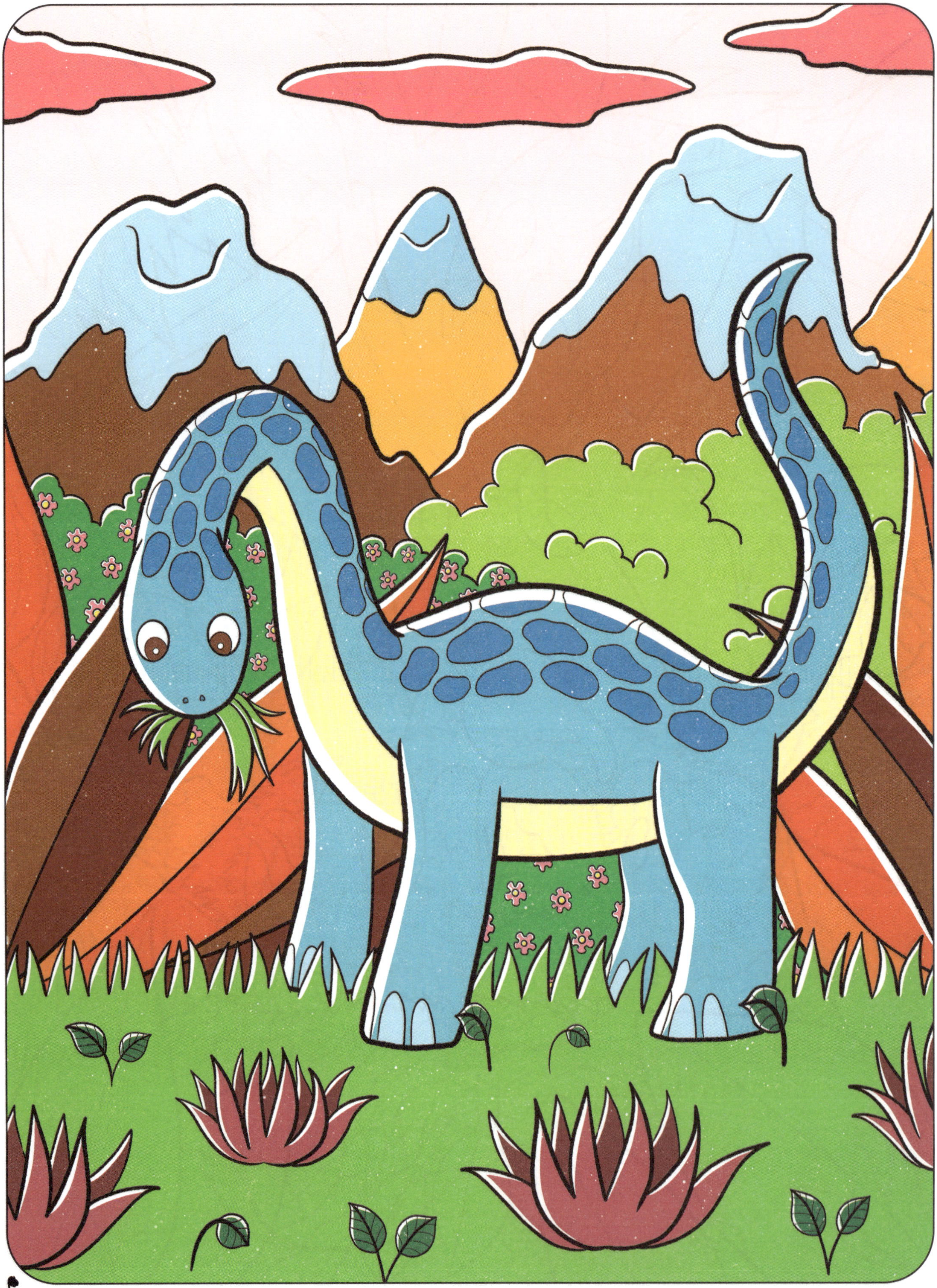

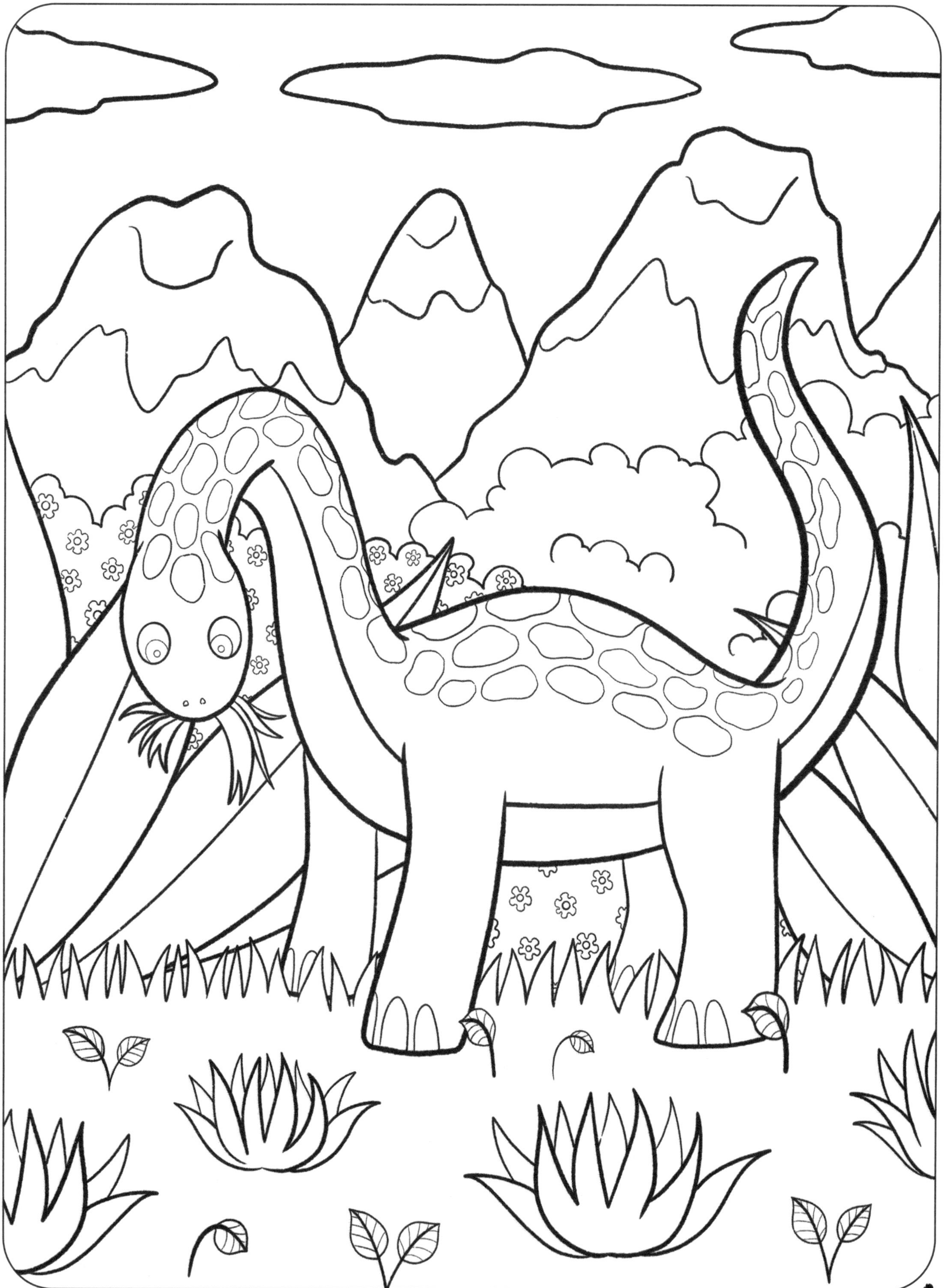

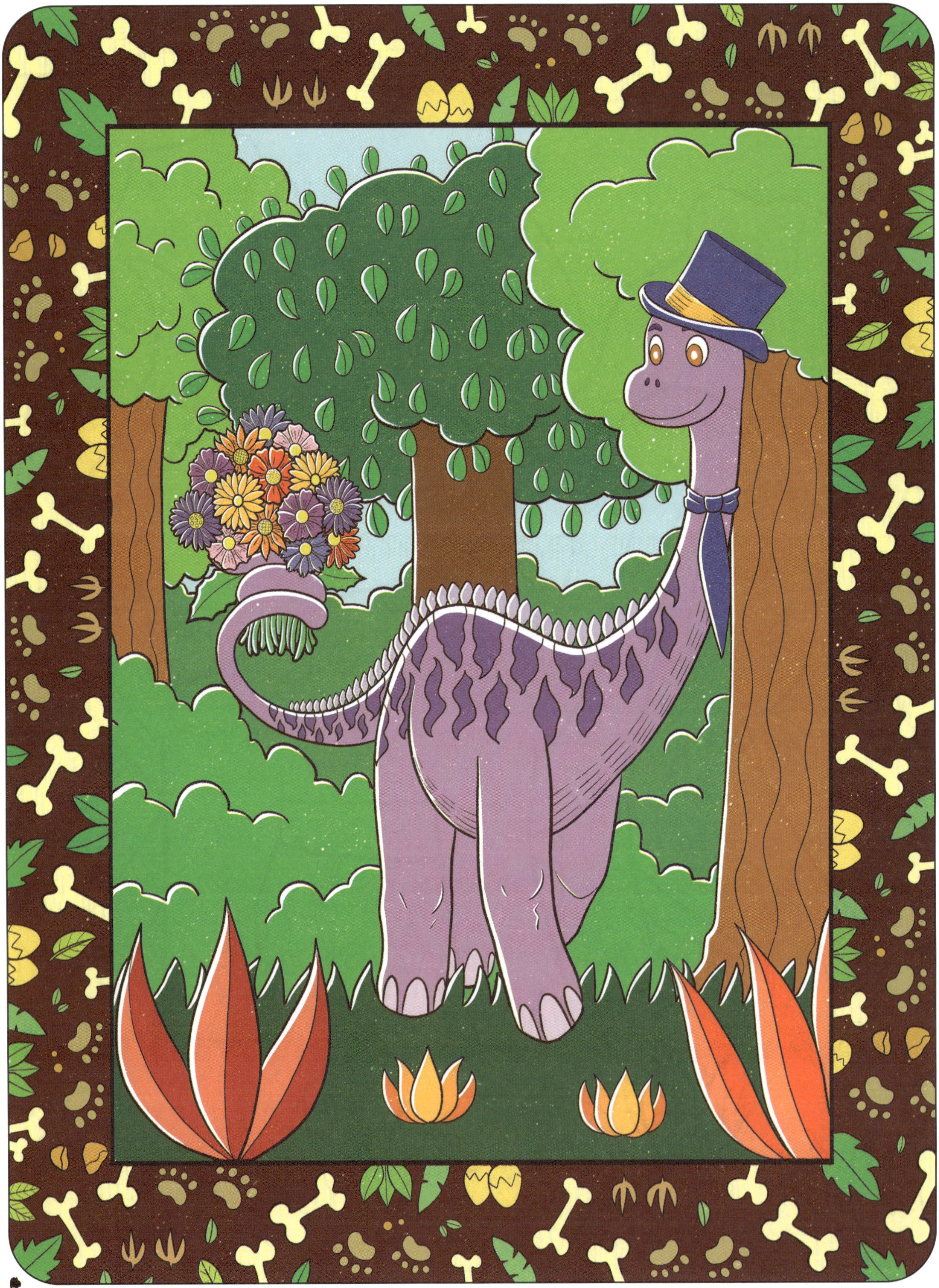

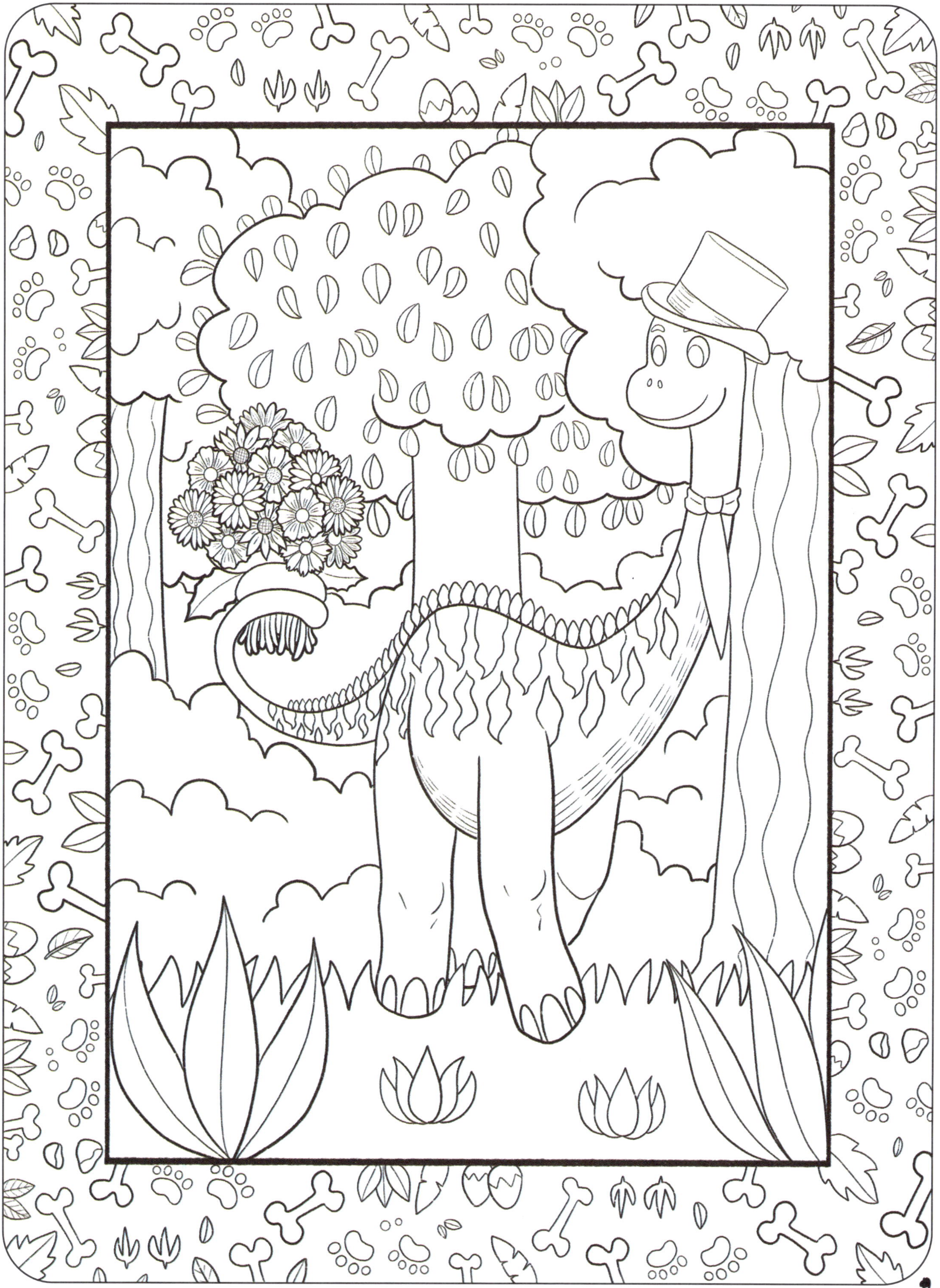

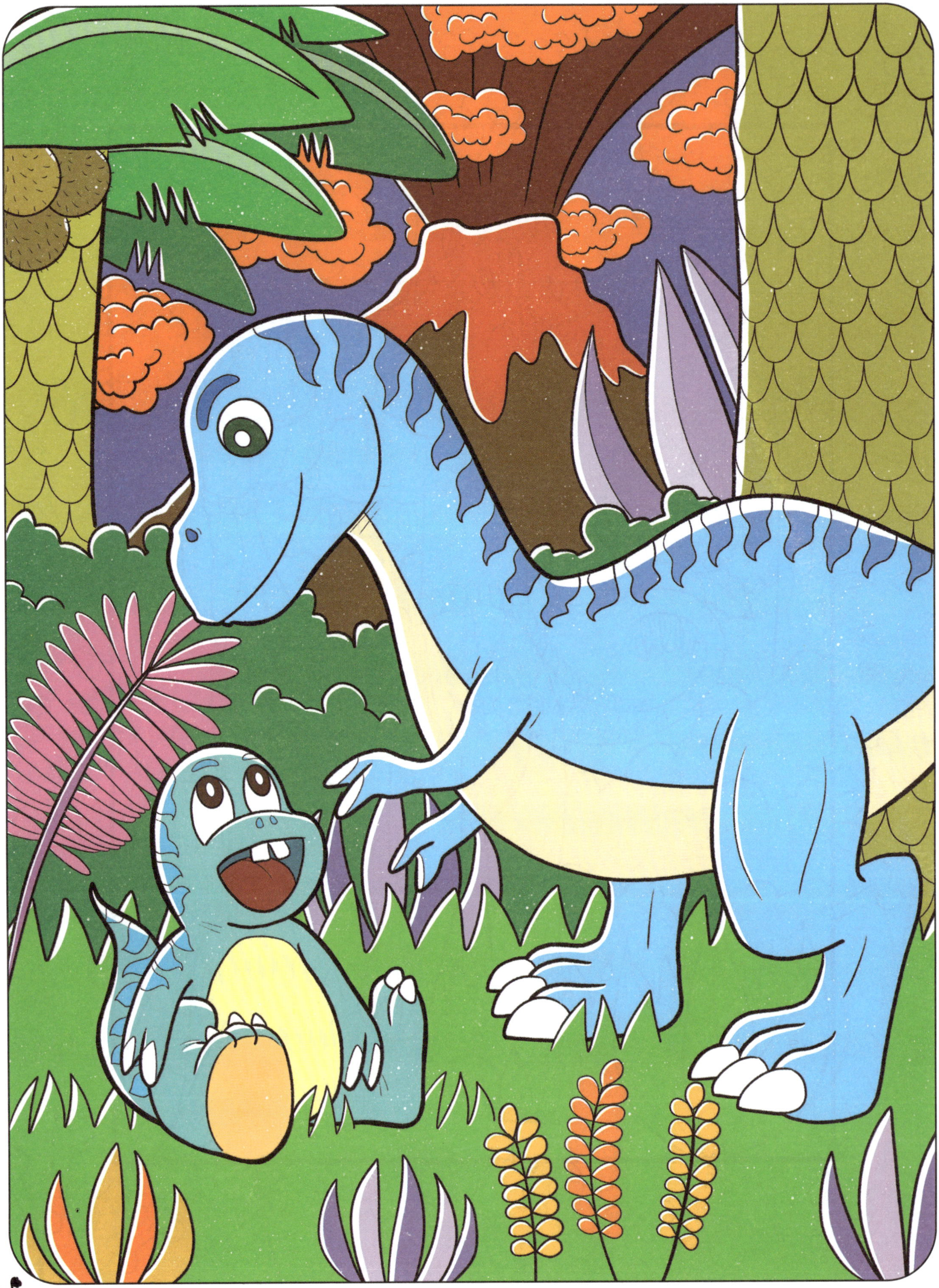

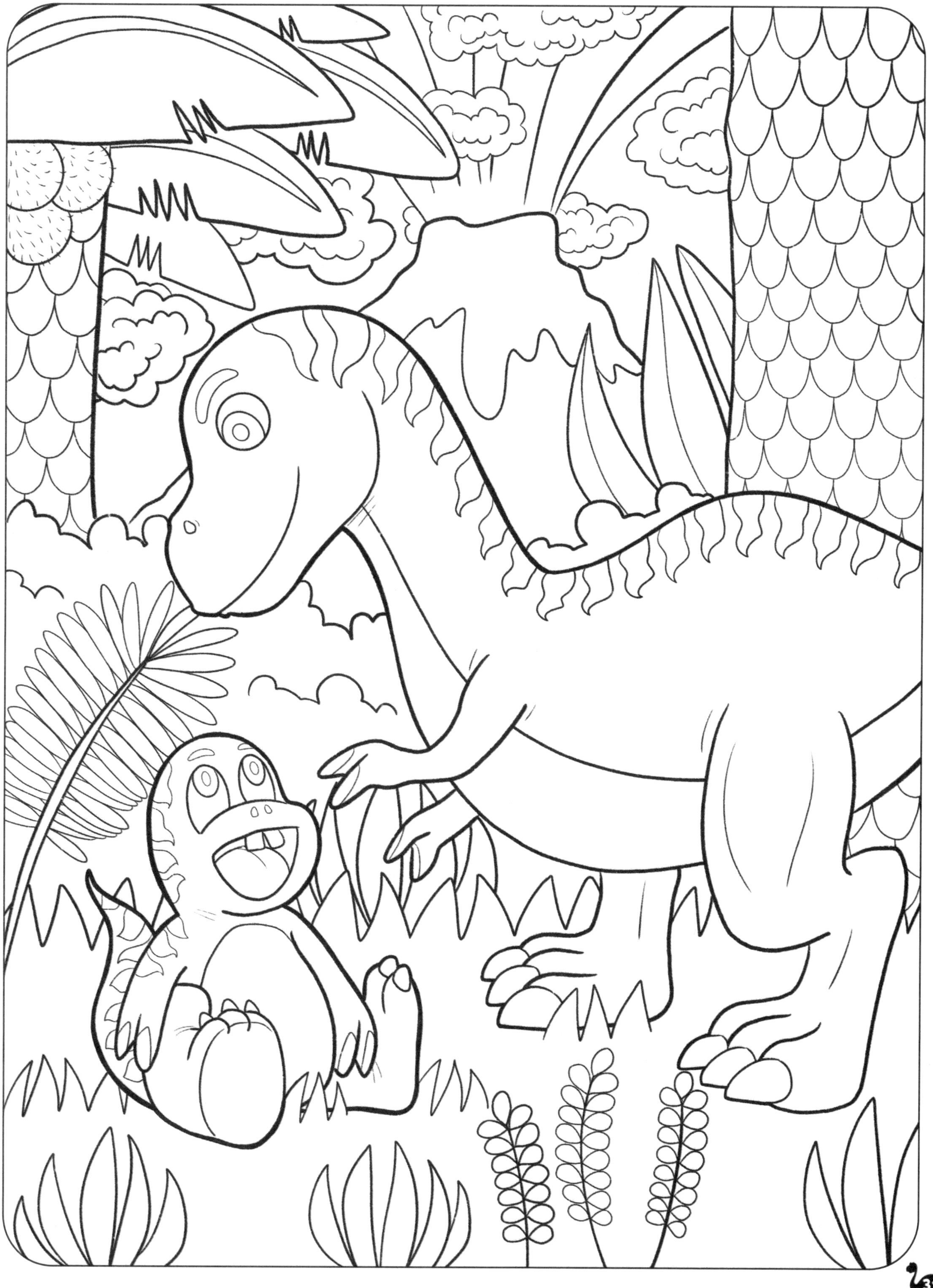

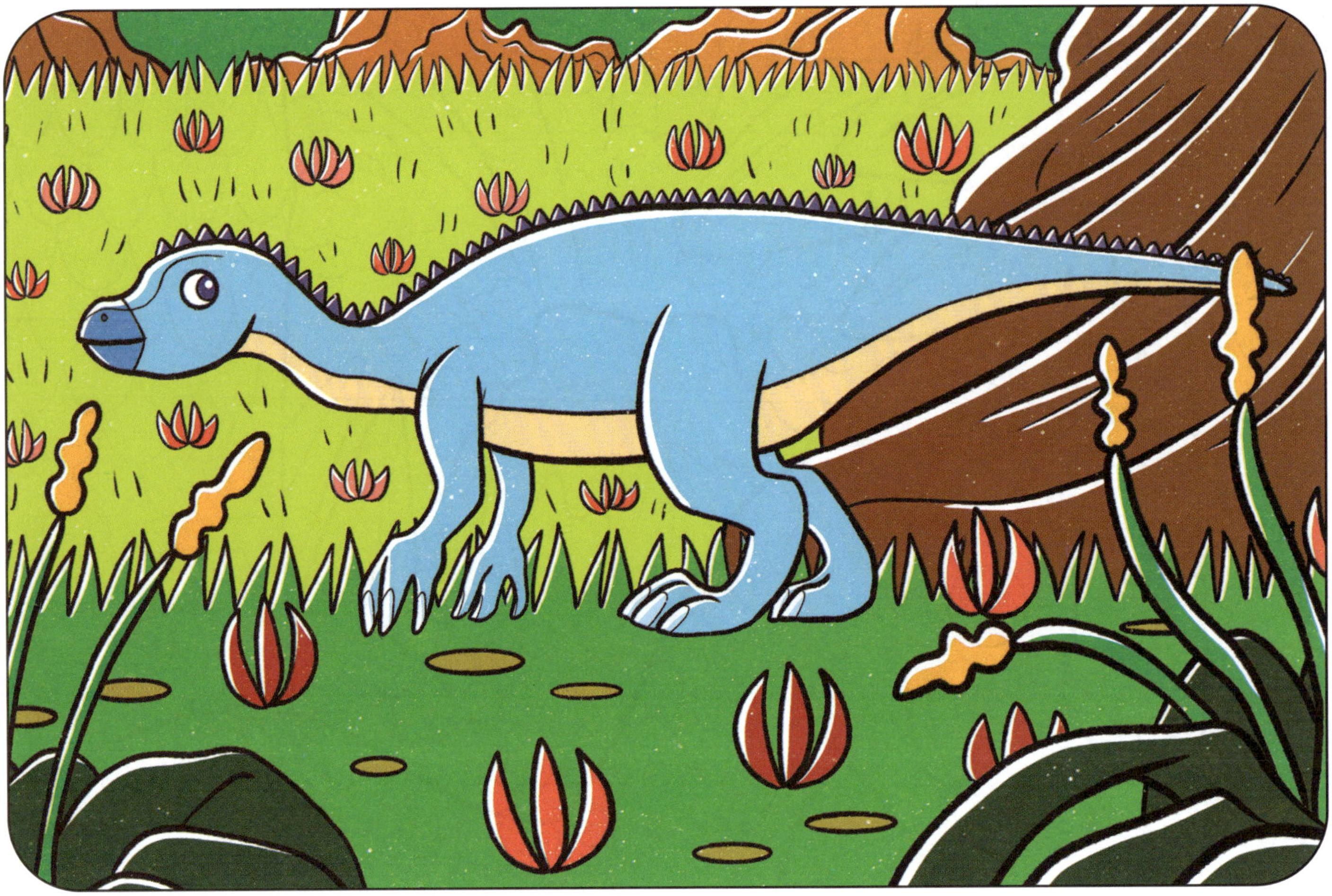

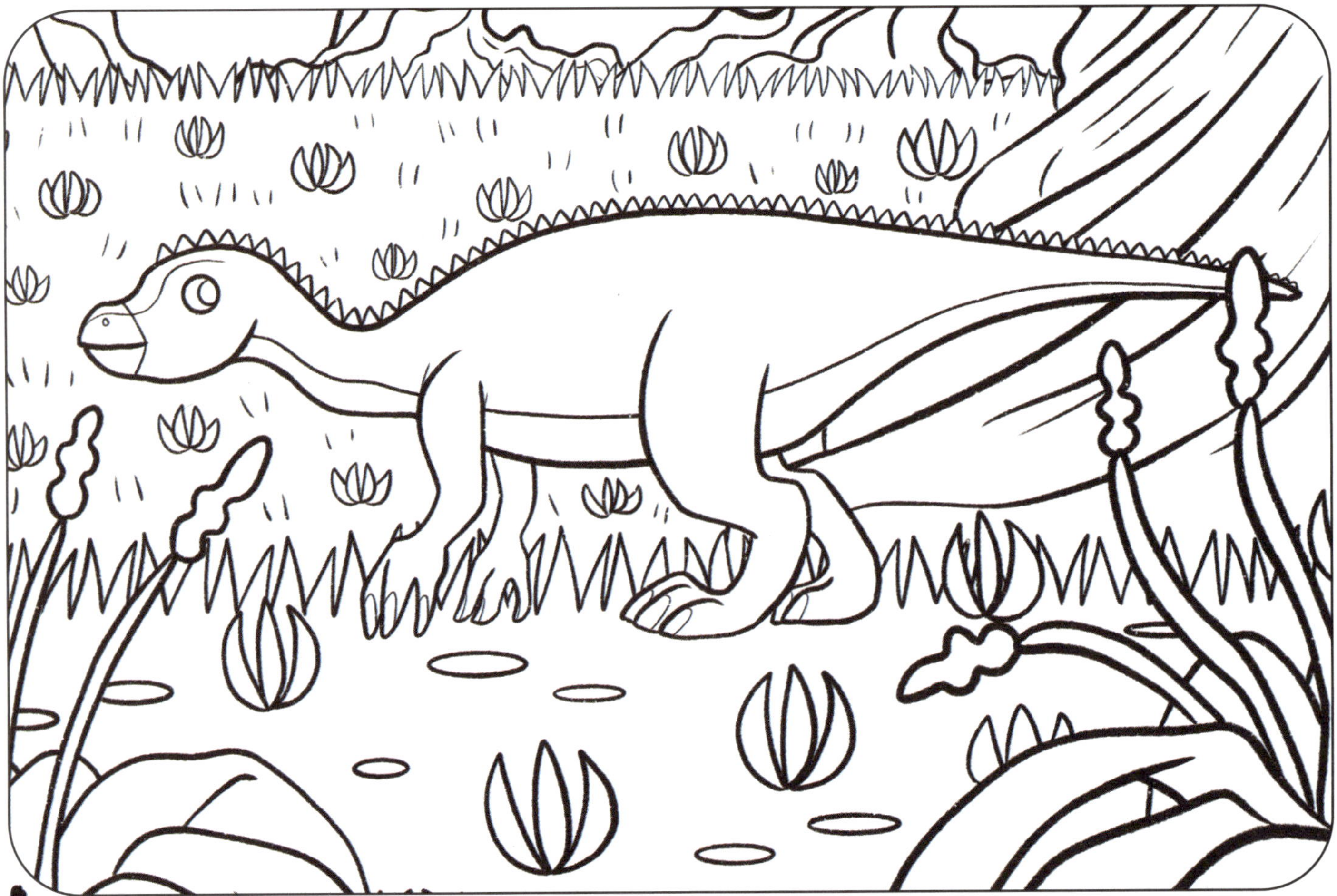